TOP-DOWN
Shawls

12 LACE-KNITTING PATTERNS

Jen Lucas

Martingale®
Create with Confidence

Top-Down Shawls: 12 Lace-Knitting Patterns
© 2018 by Jen Lucas

Martingale®
19021 120th Ave. NE, Ste. 102
Bothell, WA 98011-9511 USA
ShopMartingale.com

Printed in China
23 22 21 20 19 18   8 7 6 5 4 3 2 1

Library of Congress Cataloging-in-Publication Data is available upon request.

ISBN: 978-1-60468-960-0

MISSION STATEMENT

We empower makers who use fabric and yarn to make life more enjoyable.

CREDITS

PUBLISHER AND CHIEF VISIONARY OFFICER
Jennifer Erbe Keltner

CONTENT DIRECTOR
Karen Costello Soltys

MANAGING EDITOR
Tina Cook

ACQUISITIONS EDITOR
Amelia Johanson

TECHNICAL EDITOR
Donna Druchunas

COPY EDITOR
Kathleen Cubley

DESIGN MANAGER
Adrienne Smitke

PRODUCTION MANAGER
Regina Girard

PHOTOGRAPHER
Brent Kane

ILLUSTRATOR
Sandy Loi

Contents

Introduction

My first book, *Sock-Yarn Shawls,* was born out of something I love so much—shawls knit out of sock yarn. What started as a simple idea turned my whole life around. It helped form my business and allowed me to travel the country, teaching knitters about the things I love most: lace and shawl knitting.

In my travels for work, I've taught my class "Design Your Own Sock-Yarn Shawl" countless times. What I've learned is that knitters like you love shawls as much as I do. You enjoy knitting from patterns, but you also want to be able to take a pattern and customize it here and there. You want to repeat a chart you like for an entire shawl or omit a stitch pattern entirely. I completely get it—that's part of what I love as a designer—and I want to bring a touch of that designing fun into your life.

In this book you'll find 12 shawl patterns—all with top-down construction and interesting stitch patterns. The patterns are divided into chapters as follows.

Wedge shawls. Wedge shawls begin on page 7, and this is a great place to start, whether you're new to shawl knitting or you're looking to design your own. The top-down triangle shawl is where it all started for me. Most of the shawls from my first book, *Sock-Yarn Shawls,* were top-down triangles. In this section you will find four patterns—two that use a 2-wedge construction and two that use a 3-wedge construction. The 2-wedge shawls feature mirror-image triangles, or wedges, on each side of a central spine. In the 3-wedge shawls you'll notice an inverted triangle in the center, flanked by two mirror-image triangles.

Crescent shawls. Turn to page 29 to discover the crescent shawl, which might be my favorite of all the top-down shawl shapes. I adore the way it takes shape—growing much wider than it does deep. It's a great shawl for those of us who love to wear huge, wide shawls like scarves. You'll find four patterns in this section, all of them using traditional top-down crescent-shawl shaping.

Half-circle shawls. The half-circle shawls that begin on page 51 use the pi-shawl shaping technique developed by Elizabeth Zimmermann. I love the semicircular shawl because it stays put on your shoulders, and all the increasing happens on planned increase rows—no increases to worry about while you're working the lace patterns! In this section, you'll find four easy-to-customize patterns all using this classic shawl shape.

Design your own shawl. What makes this book different is that I've also included a "Design Your Own Shawl" section, beginning on page 67. There you'll find templates for wedge, crescent, and half-circle shawls, along with stitch patterns that you can work in any order you choose and as many times as you like.

It's a little bit like a Choose Your Own Adventure book, but with knitting! You get to decide if you want to relax and knit one of the patterns as written or take a leap and make some of the design decisions for yourself. Whatever you choose, I hope you love these shawls as much as I do.

~Jen

Lavendula

designed by the author and knit by Cathy Rusk

Skill Level: Intermediate

SHAPE: Wedge ▽

Finished Measurements:
56" × 26"

Classic lace patterns will forever remain among my favorite. The stitch patterns in this shawl are timeless and mesmerizing; I could stare at it all day.

FEATURED YARN

3 skeins of Gems Fingering from Louet (100% merino; 50 g; 185 yds) in color Lavender

MATERIALS

550 yards of fingering-weight yarn (❶)
US size 5 (3.75 mm) circular needle, 24" or longer, or size required for gauge
4 stitch markers
Tapestry needle
Blocking supplies

GAUGE

20 sts and 32 rows = 4" in St st

Gauge is not critical for this pattern, but a different gauge will affect yardage and size of shawl.

PATTERN NOTES

This is a 2-wedge shawl.

Charts are on pages 10 and 11. If you prefer to follow written instructions for the charted material, see "Written Instructions for Charts" on page 9.

If you are using stitch markers to mark each lace repeat on the charts, you'll need to rearrange your stitch markers on rows 7, 15, 23, and 31 of Chart B.

INSTRUCTIONS

Work garter tab CO (page 93) as foll: CO 3 sts. Knit 6 rows. Turn work 90° and pick up 3 sts along the edge. Turn work 90° and pick up 3 sts from CO edge—9 sts total.

Set-up row (WS): K3, P3, K3.

Row 1 (RS): K3, PM, YO, K1, YO, PM, K1, PM, YO, K1, YO, PM, K3—13 sts.

Row 2: K3, purl to last 3 sts, K3.

Row 3: K3, SM, YO, knit to marker, YO, SM, K1, SM, YO, knit to marker, YO, SM, K3—17 sts.

I love to make shawls as customizable as possible for you. You can repeat either chart as many times as you like! Note that increasing the number of chart repeats will affect yardage requirement.

Rep rows 2 and 3 another 6 times—41 sts. Rep row 2 once more.

Cont working first 3 sts and last 3 sts in garter st (knit every row). Work the center st in stockinette (knit on RS, purl on WS). Work charts on each half of shawl as foll:

Chart A 4 times—169 sts.

Chart B twice—297 sts.

FINISHING

BO loosely knitwise (page 94) on RS. Block shawl to finished measurements given at beg of patt. With tapestry needle, weave in ends.

STITCH-COUNT BREAKDOWN	
First rep of Chart A	73 sts
Second rep of Chart A	105 sts
Third rep of Chart A	137 sts
Fourth rep of Chart A	169 sts
First rep of Chart B	233 sts
Second rep of Chart B	297 sts

WRITTEN INSTRUCTIONS FOR CHARTS

If you prefer to follow written instructions rather than a chart, use the row-by-row instructions below.

Chart A

Row 1 (RS): YO, K1, *ssk, (K1, YO) twice, K1, K2tog, K1; rep from * to marker, YO.

Row 2 and all even-numbered rows (WS): Purl all sts.

Row 3: YO, K2, *ssk, (K1, YO) twice, K1, K2tog, K1; rep from * to 1 st before marker, K1, YO.

Row 5: YO, K3, *ssk, (K1, YO) twice, K1, K2tog, K1; rep from * to 2 sts before marker, K2, YO.

Row 7: YO, K4, *ssk, (K1, YO) twice, K1, K2tog, K1; rep from * to 3 sts before marker, K3, YO.

Row 9: YO, K5, *ssk, (K1, YO) twice, K1, K2tog, K1; rep from * to 4 sts before marker, K4, YO.

Row 11: YO, K3, K2tog, YO, K1, *YO, ssk, K3, K2tog, YO, K1; rep from * to 5 sts before marker, YO, ssk, K3, YO.

Row 13: YO, K3, K2tog, YO, K2, *K1, YO, ssk, K1, K2tog, YO, K2; rep from * to 6 sts before marker, K1, YO, ssk, K3, YO.

Row 15: YO, K2, YO, sk2p, YO, K3, *K2, YO, sk2p, YO, K3; rep from * to 7 sts before marker, K2, YO, sk2p, YO, K2, YO.

Row 16: Purl all sts.

Rep rows 1–16 for patt.

Chart B

Row 1 (RS): YO, K1, *K1, YO, K2tog, YO, K3, sk2p, K3, YO, ssk, YO, K2; rep from * to marker, YO.

Row 2 and all even-numbered rows (WS): Purl all sts.

Row 3: YO, K2, *ssk, (YO, K2) twice, sk2p, (K2, YO) twice, K2tog, K1; rep from * to 1 st before marker, K1, YO.

Row 5: YO, K3, *ssk, YO, K3, YO, K1, sk2p, K1, YO, K3, YO, K2tog, K1; rep from * to 2 sts before marker, K2, YO.

Row 7: YO, K2, YO, sk2p, *YO, K1, YO, ssk, K2, YO, sk2p, YO, K2, K2tog, YO, K1, YO, sk2p; rep from * to 2 sts before marker, YO, K2, YO.

Row 9: YO, K1, ssk, YO, K2, *K1, YO, K2tog, YO, K3, sk2p, K3, YO, ssk, YO, K2; rep from * to 4 sts before marker, K1, YO, K2tog, K1, YO.

Row 11: YO, K3, YO, K2tog, K1, *ssk, (YO, K2) twice, sk2p, (K2, YO) twice, K2tog, K1; rep from * to 5 sts before marker, ssk, YO, K3, YO.

Row 13: YO, K4, YO, K2tog, K1, *ssk, YO, K3, YO, K1, sk2p, K1, YO, K3, YO, K2tog, K1; rep from * to 6 sts before marker, ssk, YO, K4, YO.

Row 15: YO, K3, K2tog, YO, K1, YO, sk2p, *YO, K1, YO, ssk, K2, YO, sk2p, YO, K2, K2tog, YO, K1, YO, sk2p; rep from * to 6 sts before marker, YO, K1, YO, ssk, K3, YO.

Row 17: YO, K1, K2tog, K2, YO, ssk, YO, K2, *K1, YO, K2tog, YO, K3, sk2p, K3, YO, ssk, YO, K2; rep from * to 8 sts before marker, K1, YO, K2tog, YO, K2, ssk, K1, YO.

Row 19: YO, K1, K2tog, (K2, YO) twice, K2tog, K1, *ssk, (YO, K2) twice, sk2p, (K2, YO) twice, K2tog, K1; rep from * to 9 sts before marker, ssk, (YO, K2) twice, ssk, K1, YO.

Row 21: YO, K2, K2tog, K1, YO, K3, YO, K2tog, K1, *ssk, YO, K3, YO, K1, sk2p, K1, YO, K3, YO, K2tog, K1; rep from * to 10 sts before marker, ssk, YO, K3, YO, K1, ssk, K2, YO.

Row 23: YO, K3, K2tog, YO, K2, K2tog, YO, K1, YO, sk2p, *YO, K1, YO, ssk, K2, YO, sk2p, YO, K2, K2tog, YO, K1, YO, sk2p; rep from * to 10 sts before marker, YO, K1, YO, ssk, K2, YO, ssk, K3, YO.

Row 25: YO, K4, K2tog, K3, YO, ssk, YO, K2, *K1, YO, K2tog, YO, K3, sk2p, K3, YO, ssk, YO, K2; rep from * to 12 sts before marker, K1, YO, K2tog, YO, K3, ssk, K4, YO.

Row 27: (YO, K2) twice, sk2p, (K2, YO) twice, K2tog, K1, *ssk, (YO, K2) twice, sk2p, (K2, YO) twice, K2tog, K1; rep from * to 13 sts before marker, ssk, (YO, K2) twice, sk2p, (K2, YO) twice.

Row 29: YO, K4, YO, K1, sk2p, K1, YO, K3, YO, K2tog, K1, *ssk, YO, K3, YO, K1, sk2p, K1, YO, K3, YO, K2tog, K1; rep from * to 14 sts before marker, ssk, YO, K3, YO, K1, sk2p, K1, YO, K4, YO.

Row 31: YO, K2, YO, ssk, K2, YO, sk2p, YO, K2, K2tog, YO, K1, YO, sk2p, *YO, K1, YO, ssk, K2, YO, sk2p, YO, K2, K2tog, YO, K1, YO, sk2p; rep from * to 14 sts before marker, YO, K1, YO, ssk, K2, YO, sk2p, YO, K2, K2tog, YO, K2, YO.

Row 32: Purl all sts.

Rep rows 1–32 for patt.

Lavendula Chart A

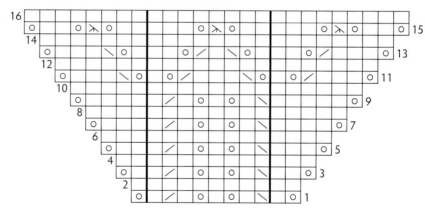

Repeat = 8 sts

Chart Legend

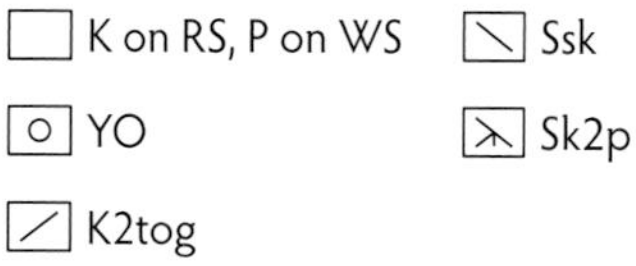

☐	K on RS, P on WS	�	Ssk
○	YO	⋏	Sk2p
╱	K2tog		

Lavendula Chart B

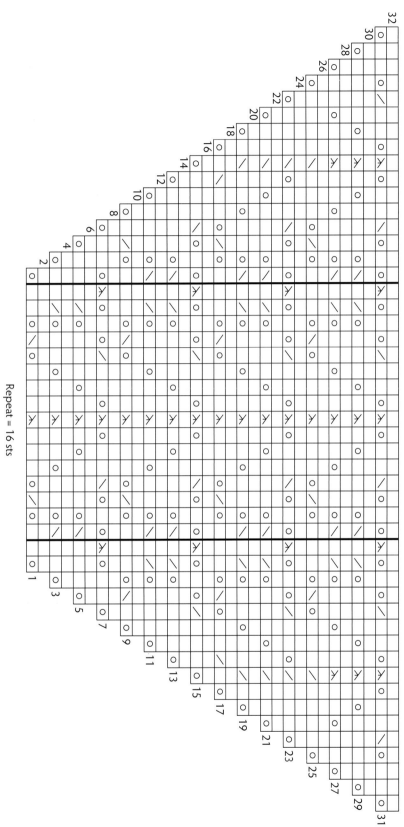

Chart Legend

☐ K on RS, P on WS	◣ Ssk
◯ YO	⋋ Sk2p
◹ K2tog	

Repeat = 16 sts

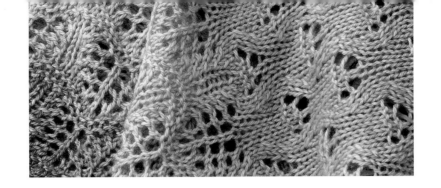

Benicia

designed and knit by the author

Skill Level: Intermediate

SHAPE: Wedge ▽

**Finished Measurements:
62" × 16"**

*Three-wedge shawls like
Benicia are ideal for a cool,
breezy day at the beach.
You can wear them in a
variety of ways, and they're
sure to stay in place and
keep you cozy and stylish
while you comb the beach
for sea glass and shells.*

FEATURED YARN

1 ball of Opulence from
KnitCircus (80% superwash
merino/10% cashmere/
10% nylon; 150 g; 660 yds)
in color Beach Glass

MATERIALS

650 yards of fingering-weight
  yarn (**1**)
US size 4 (3.50 mm) circular
  needle, 24" or longer, or
  size required for gauge
6 stitch markers
Tapestry needle
Blocking supplies

GAUGE

18 sts and 36 rows = 4" in St st

Gauge is not critical for this
pattern, but a different gauge
will affect yardage and size
of shawl.

PATTERN NOTES

This is a 3-wedge shawl.

Charts are on page 17. If you
prefer to follow written
instructions for the charted
material, see "Written
Instructions for Charts" on
page 14.

INSTRUCTIONS

**Work garter tab CO (page 93)
as foll:** CO 3 sts. Knit 10 rows.
Turn work 90° and pick up 5
sts along the edge. Turn work
90° and pick up 3 sts from CO
edge—11 sts total.

Set-up row (WS): K3, P5, K3.

Row 1 (RS): K3, (PM, YO, K1,
YO, PM, K1) twice, PM, YO, K1,
YO, PM, K3—17 sts.

Row 2: K3, purl to last 3
sts, K3.

Row 3: K3, (SM, YO, knit to
next marker, YO, SM, K1)
twice, SM, YO, knit to last
marker, YO, SM, K3—23 sts.

Rep rows 2 and 3 another 4
times—47 sts. Rep row 2
once more.

The feather-and-fan detail at the edge of the shawl adds to the beachy vibe of this piece. ▶

Body of Shawl

For the remainder of the shawl, slip the stitch markers on every row. Cont working the first 3 sts and last 3 sts in garter st (knit every row) and the 2 spine sts (the single st marked with a st marker on each side) in St st (knit on RS, purl on WS). On each of the 3 wedges (starting with 13 sts in each section), in between the stitch markers, work charts as foll:

Chart A 3 times—263 sts.

Chart B twice—407 sts.

Make It Your Own!

You can repeat either chart as many times as you like. Note that changing the number of times you repeat the charts will affect the yardage requirement.

STITCH-COUNT BREAKDOWN	
First rep of Chart A	119 sts
Second rep of Chart A	191 sts
Third rep of Chart A	263 sts
First rep of Chart B	335 sts
Second rep of Chart B	407 sts

FINISHING

BO loosely knitwise (page 94) on RS. Block shawl to finished measurements given at beg of patt. With tapestry needle, weave in ends.

WRITTEN INSTRUCTIONS FOR CHARTS

If you prefer to follow written instructions rather than a chart, use the row-by-row instructions that follow.

◀ *There are so many ways to wear 3-wedge shawls. I particularly love to wear them this way—almost like a scarf or cowl.*

Chart A

Row 1 (RS): YO, K1, *K2, K2tog, (K1, YO) twice, K1, ssk, K3; rep from * to marker, YO.

Row 2 (WS): P1, *P5, K3, P4; rep from * to 2 sts before marker, P2.

Row 3: YO, K2, *K1, K2tog, K1, YO, K3, YO, K1, ssk, K2; rep from * to 1 st before marker, K1, YO.

Row 4: P2, *P4, K5, P3; rep from * to 3 sts before marker, P3.

Row 5: YO, knit to marker, YO.

Row 6: Purl all sts.

Row 7: YO, K2tog, K1, YO, K1, *YO, K1, ssk, K5, K2tog, K1, YO, K1; rep from * to 3 sts before marker, YO, K1, ssk, YO.

Row 8: P3, K1, *K2, P9, K1; rep from * to 5 sts before marker, K2, P3.

Row 9: YO, K2tog, K1, YO, K2, *K1, YO, K1, ssk, K3, K2tog, K1, YO, K2; rep from * to 4 sts before marker, K1, YO, K1, ssk, YO.

Row 10: P3, K2, *K3, P7, K2; rep from * to 6 sts before marker, K3, P3.

Rows 11 and 12: Rep rows 5 and 6.

Row 13: (YO, K1) twice, ssk, K3, *K2, K2tog, (K1, YO) twice, K1, ssk, K3; rep from * to 6 sts before marker, K2, K2tog, (K1, YO) twice.

Row 14: P1, K2, P4, *P5, K3, P4; rep from * to 8 sts before marker, P5, K2, P1.

Row 15: YO, K3, YO, K1, ssk, K2, *K1, K2tog, K1, YO, K3, YO, K1, ssk, K2; rep from * to 7 sts before marker, K1, K2tog, K1, YO, K3, YO.

Row 5: YO, K3, *K2tog twice, (YO, K1) 3 times, YO, ssk twice, K1; rep from * to 2 sts before marker, K2, YO.

Row 7: YO, K4, *K2tog twice, (YO, K1) 3 times, YO, ssk twice, K1; rep from * to 3 sts before marker, K3, YO.

Row 9: YO, knit to marker, YO.

Row 10: Knit all sts.

Rows 11 and 12: Rep rows 9 and 10.

Row 13: (YO, K1) twice, YO, ssk twice, K1, *K2tog twice, (YO, K1) 3 times, YO, ssk twice, K1; rep from * to 6 sts before marker, K2tog twice, (YO, K1) twice, YO.

Row 15: YO, K2, YO, K1, YO, ssk twice, K1, *K2tog twice, (YO, K1) 3 times, YO, ssk twice, K1; rep from * to 7 sts before marker, K2tog twice, YO, K1, YO, K2, YO.

Row 17: YO, K3, YO, K1, YO, ssk twice, K1, *K2tog twice, (YO, K1) 3 times, YO, ssk twice, K1; rep from * to 8 sts before marker, K2tog twice, YO, K1, YO, K3, YO.

Row 19: YO, K1, K2tog, (YO, K1) twice, YO, ssk twice, K1, *K2tog twice, (YO, K1) 3 times, YO, ssk twice, K1; rep from * to 9 sts before marker, K2tog twice, (YO, K1) twice, YO, ssk, K1, YO.

Rows 21–24: Rep rows 9 and 10 twice.

Rep rows 1–24 for patt.

Row 16: P1, K4, P3, *P4, K5, P3; rep from * to 9 sts before marker, P4, K4, P1.

Rows 17 and 18: Rep rows 5 and 6.

Row 19: YO, K6, K2tog, K1, YO, K1, *YO, K1, ssk, K5, K2tog, K1, YO, K1; rep from * to 9 sts before marker, YO, K1, ssk, K6, YO.

Row 20: P9, K1, *K2, P9, K1; rep from * to 11 sts before marker, K2, P9.

Row 21: YO, K6, K2tog, K1, YO, K2, *K1, YO, K1, ssk, K3, K2tog, K1, YO, K2; rep from * to 10 sts before marker, K1, YO, K1, ssk, K6, YO.

Row 22: P9, K2, *K3, P7, K2; rep from * to 12 sts before marker, K3, P9.

Rows 23 and 24: Rep rows 5 and 6.

Rep rows 1–24 for patt.

Chart B

Row 1 (RS): YO, K1, *K2tog twice, (YO, K1) 3 times, YO, ssk twice, K1; rep from * to marker, YO.

Rows 2, 4, 6, 8, 14, 16, 18, and 20 (WS): Purl all sts.

Row 3: YO, K2, *K2tog twice, (YO, K1) 3 times, YO, ssk twice, K1; rep from * to 1 st before marker, K1, YO.

Top-Down Shawls

Benicia Chart A

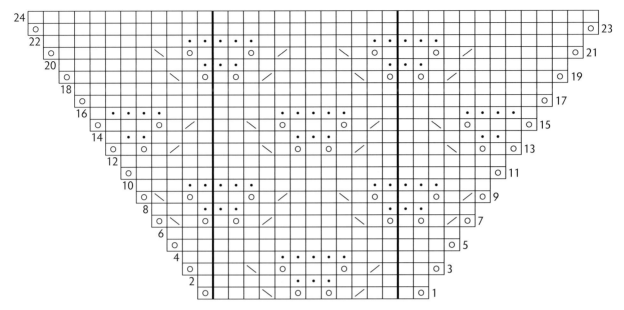

Repeat = 12 sts

Benicia Chart B

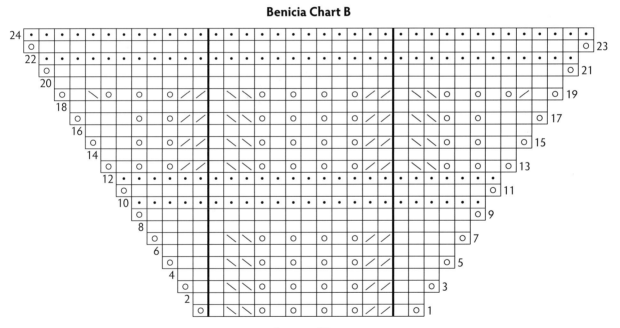

Repeat = 12 sts

Chart Legend

☐ K on RS, P on WS	╱ K2tog
☒ P on RS, K on WS	╲ Ssk
⊡ YO	

Kokedama

designed and knit by the author

Skill Level: Intermediate

SHAPE: Wedge ▽

Finished Measurements:
64" × 30"

Kokedama is a combination of everything that makes me happy when it comes to knitting. A beautiful, airy yarn; simple stockinette stitch; and a showstopping leaf-lace pattern make this piece a trifecta of joy.

FEATURED YARN

1 skein of Cloud from Anzula Luxury Fibers (80% superwash merino/10% cashmere/10% nylon; 113 g; 575 yds) in color Hibiscus

MATERIALS

575 yards of light fingering-weight yarn (1)
US size 3 (3.25 mm) circular needle, 24" or longer, or size required for gauge
4 stitch markers
Tapestry needle
Blocking supplies

GAUGE

18 sts and 32 rows = 4" in St st

Gauge is not critical for this pattern, but a different gauge will affect yardage and size of shawl.

PATTERN NOTES

This is a 2-wedge shawl.

Charts are on page 22. If you prefer to follow written instructions for the charted material, see "Written Instructions for Charts" on page 21.

If you are using stitch markers to mark each 16-stitch lace repeat on the charts, you'll need to rearrange your stitch markers on rows 1, 3, 5, and 7 of Chart B.

INSTRUCTIONS

Work garter tab CO (page 93) as foll: CO 3 sts. Knit 6 rows. Turn work 90° and pick up 3 sts along the edge. Turn work 90° and pick up 3 sts from CO edge—9 sts total.

Set-up row (WS): K3, P3, K3.

Row 1 (RS): K3, PM, YO, K1, YO, PM, K1, PM, YO, K1, YO, PM, K3—13 sts.

Row 2: K3, purl to last 3 sts, K3.

Row 3: K3, SM, YO, knit to marker, YO, SM, K1, SM, YO, knit to marker, YO, SM, K3—17 sts.

Rep rows 2 and 3 another 54 times—233 sts. Rep row 2 once more.

Cont working first 3 sts and last 3 sts in garter st (knit every row). Work the center st in stockinette (knit on RS, purl on WS). In between st markers, work charts on each half of shawl as foll:

Chart A 5 times—393 sts.

Chart B once—409 sts.

Make It Your Own!

You can repeat Chart A as many times as you like before moving on to Chart B. Note that changing the number of times you repeat Chart A will affect the yardage requirement.

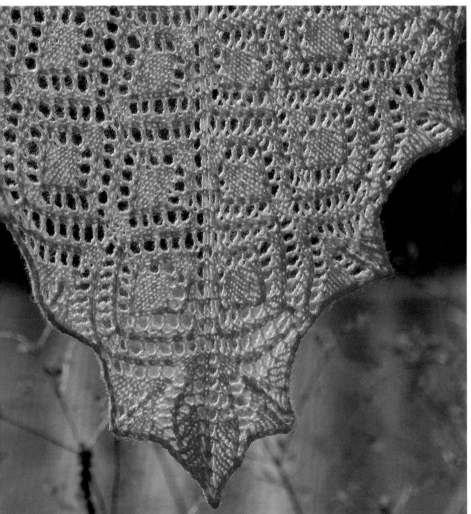

◀ *The geometric leaf pattern at the edge of this accessory makes for an enjoyable challenge after working the simple body.*

STITCH-COUNT BREAKDOWN	
First rep of Chart A	265 sts
Second rep of Chart A	297 sts
Third rep of Chart A	329 sts
Fourth rep of Chart A	361 sts
Fifth rep of Chart A	393 sts
Chart B	409 sts

FINISHING

BO loosely knitwise (page 94) on WS. Block shawl to finished measurements given at beg of patt. With tapestry needle, weave in ends.

WRITTEN INSTRUCTIONS FOR CHARTS

If you prefer to follow written instructions rather than a chart, use the row-by-row instructions below.

Chart A

Row 1 (RS): YO, K1, *YO, ssk, K1, YO, ssk, K5, (K2tog, YO, K1) twice; rep from * to marker, YO.

Row 2 and all even-numbered rows (WS): Purl all sts.

Row 3: YO, K2, *(K1, YO, ssk) twice, K3, K2tog, YO, K1, K2tog, YO, K2; rep from * to 1 st before marker, K1, YO.

Row 5: YO, K3, *K2, (YO, ssk, K1) twice, K2tog, YO, K1, K2tog, YO, K3; rep from * to 2 sts before marker, K2, YO.

Row 7: YO, K1, K2tog, YO, K1, *(YO, ssk, K1) twice, YO, sk2p, (YO, K1, K2tog) twice, YO, K1; rep from * to 3 sts before marker, YO, ssk, K1, YO.

Row 9: YO, K1, YO, K2tog, YO, K2, *(K1, YO, ssk) twice, K3, K2tog, YO, K1, K2tog, YO, K2; rep from * to 4 sts before marker, K1, YO, ssk, YO, K1, YO.

Row 11: YO, K2, YO, K2tog, YO, K3, *K2, (YO, ssk, K1) twice, K2tog, YO, K1, K2tog, YO, K3; rep from * to 6 sts before marker, K2, YO, ssk, YO, K2, YO.

Row 12: Purl all sts.

Rep rows 1–12 for patt.

Chart B

Row 1 (RS): YO, K3, K2tog, YO, K2, YO, cdd, *YO, K2, YO, ssk, K1, YO, sk2p, YO, K1, K2tog, YO, K2, YO, cdd; rep from * to 7 sts before marker, YO, K2, YO, ssk, K3, YO.

Row 2 and all even-numbered rows (WS): Purl all sts.

Row 3: YO, K3, K2tog, YO, K3, YO, cdd, *YO, K3, YO, ssk, YO, cdd, YO, K2tog, YO, K3, YO, cdd; rep from * to 8 sts before marker, YO, K3, YO, ssk, K3, YO.

Row 5: YO, K2, *K1, K2tog, YO, K4, YO, cdd, YO, K4, YO, ssk; rep from * to 3 sts before marker, K3, YO.

Row 7: YO, K3, K2tog, YO, K5, YO, cdd, *YO, K5, YO, sk2p, YO, K5, YO, cdd; rep from * to 10 sts before marker, YO, K5, YO, ssk, K3, YO.

Kokedama Chart A

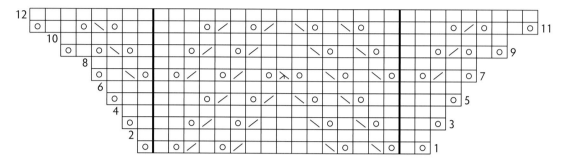

Repeat = 16 sts

Chart Legend

☐ K on RS, P on WS	╲ Ssk
⊙ YO	⋋ Sk2p
╱ K2tog	

Kokedama Chart B

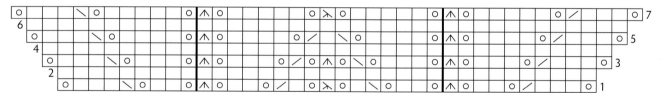

Repeat = 16 sts

Chart Legend

☐ K on RS, P on WS	╲ Ssk
⊙ YO	⋋ Sk2p
╱ K2tog	⋀ Cdd

Pekara

designed by the author and knit by Jenni Lesniak

Skill Level: Intermediate

SHAPE: Wedge ▽

Finished Measurements:
54" × 17"

When I saw that the colorway of this yarn is named after a Chicago suburb where I spent a lot of time in my early adult years—Buffalo Grove—I had to pick it. Pekara's geometric lace pattern is neat and orderly, reminiscent of my days working in a laboratory near Buffalo Grove.

FEATURED YARN

3 skeins of Shepherd Sport from Lorna's Laces (100% superwash merino; 57 g; 200 yds) in color Buffalo Grove

MATERIALS

600 yards of sport-weight yarn **2**

US size 6 (4.00 mm) circular needle, 24" or longer, or size required for gauge
6 stitch markers
Tapestry needle
Blocking supplies

GAUGE

24 sts and 28 rows = 4" in St st

Gauge is not critical for this pattern, but a different gauge will affect yardage and size of shawl.

PATTERN NOTES

This is a 3-wedge shawl.

Charts are on pages 27 and 28. If you prefer to follow written instructions for the charted material, see "Written Instructions for Charts" on page 25.

INSTRUCTIONS

Work garter tab CO (page 93) as foll: CO 3 sts. Knit 10 rows. Turn work 90° and pick up 5 sts along the edge. Turn work 90° and pick up 3 sts from CO edge—11 sts total.

Set-up row (WS): K3, P5, K3.

Row 1 (RS): K3, (PM, YO, K1, YO, PM, K1) twice, PM, YO, K1, YO, PM, K3—17 sts.

Row 2: K3, purl to last 3 sts, K3.

Row 3: K3, (SM, YO, knit to the next marker, YO, SM, K1) twice, SM, YO, knit to last marker, YO, SM, K3—23 sts.

Rep rows 2 and 3 another 5 times—53 sts. Rep row 2 once more.

Body of Shawl

For the remainder of the shawl, slip the stitch markers on every row. Cont working the first 3 sts and last 3 sts in garter st (knit every row) and the 2 spine sts (i.e. the single st marked with a st marker on each side) in St st (knit on RS, purl on WS). On each of the 3 wedges (starting with 15 sts in each section), in between the stitch markers, work charts as foll:

Work Chart A 3 times—269 sts.

Work Chart B twice—413 sts.

Work Chart C once—443 sts.

STITCH-COUNT BREAKDOWN	
First rep of Chart A	125 sts
Second rep of Chart A	197 sts
Third rep of Chart A	269 sts
First rep of Chart B	341 sts
Second rep of Chart B	413 sts
Chart C	443 sts

Make It Your Own!

It's easy to adjust the size of this shawl. You can add extra repeats of Chart A or B or both, as desired, before finishing your shawl with Chart C. Note that changing the number of times you repeat the charts will affect the yardage requirement.

FINISHING

BO loosely knitwise (page 94) on WS. Block shawl to finished measurements given at beg of patt. With tapestry needle, weave in ends.

WRITTEN INSTRUCTIONS FOR CHARTS

If you prefer to follow written instructions rather than a chart, use the row-by-row instructions that follow.

Chart A

Row 1 (RS): YO, K2, *YO, ssk, K7, K2tog, YO, K1; rep from * to 1 st before marker, K1, YO.

Row 2 and all even-numbered rows (WS): Purl all sts.

Row 3: YO, K3, *YO, K1, ssk, K5, K2tog, K1, YO, K1; rep from * to 2 sts before marker, K2, YO.

Row 5: YO, K1, K2tog, YO, K1, *YO, K2, ssk, K3, K2tog, K2, YO, K1; rep from * to 3 sts before marker, YO, ssk, K1, YO.

Row 7: YO, K1, K2tog, K1, YO, K1, *YO, K3, ssk, K1, K2tog, K3, YO, K1; rep from * to 4 sts before marker, YO, K1, ssk, K1, YO.

Row 9: YO, K1, K2tog, K2, YO, K1, *YO, K4, sk2p, K4, YO, K1; rep from * to 5 sts before marker, YO, K2, ssk, K1, YO.

Row 11: YO, K4, K2tog, YO, K1, *YO, ssk, K7, K2tog, YO, K1; rep from * to 6 sts before marker, YO, ssk, K4, YO.

Row 13: YO, K4, K2tog, K1, YO, K1, *YO, K1, ssk, K5, K2tog, K1, YO, K1; rep from * to 7 sts before marker, YO, K1, ssk, K4, YO.

Row 15: YO, K4, K2tog, K2, YO, K1, *YO, K2, ssk, K3, K2tog, K2, YO, K1; rep from * to 8 sts before marker, YO, K2, ssk, K4, YO.

Row 17: YO, K1, YO, K3, K2tog, K3, YO, K1, *YO, K3, ssk, K1, K2tog, K3, YO, K1; rep from * to 9 sts before marker, YO, K3, ssk, K3, YO, K1, YO.

Row 19: YO, K1, YO, K4, K2tog, K4, YO, K1, *YO, K4, sk2p, K4, YO, K1; rep from * to 11 sts before marker, YO, K4, ssk, K4, YO, K1, YO.

Row 20: Purl all sts.

Rep rows 1–20 for patt.

Chart B

Row 1 (RS): YO, K2, *YO, K4, cdd, K4, YO, K1; rep from * to 1 st before marker, K1, YO.

Row 2 and all even-numbered rows (WS): Purl all sts.

Row 3: YO, K3, *YO, K4, cdd, K4, YO, K1; rep from * to 2 sts before marker, K2, YO.

Row 5: YO, K1, K2tog, YO, K1, *YO, K4, cdd, K4, YO, K1; rep from * to 3 sts before marker, YO, ssk, K1, YO.

Row 7: YO, K1, K2tog, K1, YO, K1, *YO, K4, cdd, K4, YO, K1; rep from * to 4 sts before marker, YO, K1, ssk, K1, YO.

◀ *The vertical columns in the stitch pattern combined with the 3-wedge shawl construction give the piece an appealing layer of dimension.*

Row 9: YO, K1, K2tog, K2, YO, K1, *YO, K4, cdd, K4, YO, K1; rep from * to 5 sts before marker, YO, K2, ssk, K1, YO.

Row 11: YO, K1, K2tog, K3, YO, K1, *YO, K4, cdd, K4, YO, K1; rep from * to 6 sts before marker, YO, K3, ssk, K1, YO.

Row 13: YO, K1, K2tog, K4, YO, K1, *YO, K4, cdd, K4, YO, K1; rep from * to 7 sts before marker, YO, K4, ssk, K1, YO.

Row 15: YO, K2, K2tog, K4, YO, K1, *YO, K4, cdd, K4, YO, K1; rep from * to 8 sts before marker, YO, K4, ssk, K2, YO.

Row 17: YO, K1, YO, K2, K2tog, K4, YO, K1, *YO, K4, cdd, K4, YO, K1; rep from * to 9 sts before marker, YO, K4, ssk, K2, YO, K1, YO.

Row 19: YO, K1, YO, K4, K2tog, K4, YO, K1, *YO, K4, cdd, K4, YO, K1; rep from * to 11 sts before marker, YO, K4, ssk, K4, YO, K1, YO.

Row 20: Purl all sts.

Rep rows 1–20 for patt.

Chart C

Row 1 (RS): YO, K2, *YO, K4, cdd, K4, YO, K1; rep from * to 1 st before marker, K1, YO.

Row 2 and all even-numbered rows (WS): Purl all sts.

Row 3: YO, K3, *K1, YO, K3, cdd, K3, YO, K2; rep from * to 2 sts before marker, K2, YO.

Row 5: YO, K1, K2tog, YO, K1, *YO, ssk, YO, K2, cdd, K2, YO, K2tog, YO, K1; rep from * to 3 sts before marker, YO, ssk, K1, YO.

Row 7: YO, K1, K2tog, YO, K2, *K1, YO, ssk, YO, K1, cdd, K1, YO, K2tog, YO, K2; rep from * to 4 sts before marker, K1, YO, ssk, K1, YO.

Row 9: YO, K1, (K2tog, YO) twice, K1, *(YO, ssk) twice, YO, cdd, (YO, K2tog) twice, YO, K1; rep from * to 5 sts before marker, (YO, ssk) twice, K1, YO.

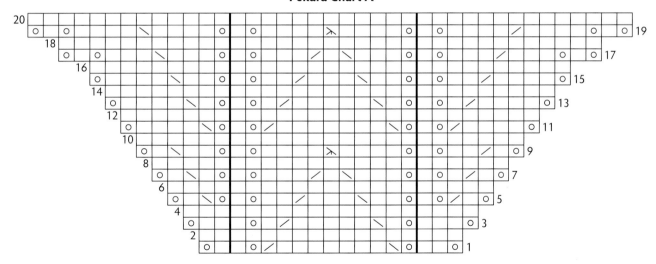

Pekara Chart A

Repeat = 12 sts

Chart Legend

☐ K on RS, P on WS   ◿ Ssk

◉ YO   ⋉ Sk2p

◺ K2tog

Pekara Chart B

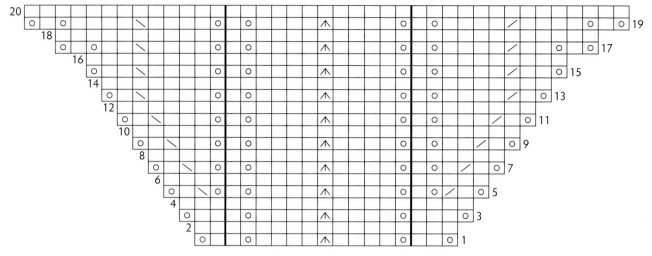

Repeat = 12 sts

Chart Legend

☐ K on RS, P on WS	◣ Ssk
◉ YO	⋀ Cdd
◢ K2tog	

Pekara Chart C

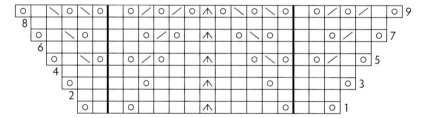

Repeat = 12 sts

Chart Legend

☐ K on RS, P on WS	◣ Ssk
◉ YO	⋀ Cdd
◢ K2tog	

Moyashi

designed by the author and knit by Rachel Brown

Skill Level: Intermediate

SHAPE: Crescent ◡

Finished Measurements:
62" × 15"

Maybe it's my math brain, but there's something I love about a shawl that features a geometric lace pattern. Funky chevrons combined with a simple vertical lace pattern along the edge of Moyashi make this math nerd happy!

FEATURED YARN

2 skeins of Sprout DK from The Fiber Seed (90% superwash merino/10% nylon; 100 g; 225 yds) in color French Rose

MATERIALS

450 yards of DK-weight yarn (3)
US size 6 (4.00 mm) circular needle, 24" or longer, or size required for gauge
Tapestry needle
Blocking supplies

GAUGE

16 sts and 26 rows = 4" in St st

Gauge is not critical for this pattern, but a different gauge will affect yardage and size of shawl.

PATTERN NOTES

Charts are on page 33. If you prefer to follow written instructions for the charted material, see "Written Instructions for Charts" on page 31.

INSTRUCTIONS

Work garter tab CO (page 93) as foll: CO 2 sts. Knit 18 rows. Turn work 90° and pick up 9 sts along the edge. Turn work 90° and pick up 2 sts from CO edge—13 sts total.

Set-up row (WS): K3, (YO, K1) to the last 3 sts, YO, K3—21 sts.

Work Chart A 6 times—201 sts.

Work Chart B 3 times—291 sts.

STITCH-COUNT BREAKDOWN	
First rep of Chart A	51 sts
Second rep of Chart A	81 sts
Third rep of Chart A	111 sts
Fourth rep of Chart A	141 sts
Fifth rep of Chart A	171 sts
Sixth rep of Chart A	201 sts
First rep of Chart B	231 sts
Second rep of Chart B	261 sts
Third rep of Chart B	291 sts

FINISHING

BO loosely knitwise (page 94) on RS. Block shawl to finished measurements given at beg of patt. With tapestry needle, weave in ends.

WRITTEN INSTRUCTIONS FOR CHARTS

If you prefer to follow written instructions rather than a chart, use the row-by-row instructions that follow.

Chart A

Row 1 (RS): K2, YO, K1, YO, *K1, YO, K5, cdd, K5, YO, K1; rep from * to last 3 sts, YO, K1, YO, K2.

Rows 2, 4, and 6 (WS): K3, YO, K1, purl to last 4 sts, K1, YO, K3.

Row 3: K2, YO, K1, YO, K3, *K1, YO, K5, cdd, K5, YO, K1; rep from * to last 6 sts, K3, YO, K1, YO, K2.

◀ *A vertical lace edging is a great way to finish a top-down shawl.*

Row 5: K2, YO, K1, YO, K6, *K1, YO, K5, cdd, K5, YO, K1; rep from * to last 9 sts, K6, YO, K1, YO, K2.

Row 7: K2, YO, K1, YO, knit to last 3 sts, YO, K1, YO, K2.

Row 8: K3, YO, knit to last 3 sts, YO, K3.

Rows 9 and 10: Rep rows 7 and 8.

Rep rows 1–10 for patt.

Chart B

Row 1 (RS): K2, YO, K1, YO, *K1, YO, cdd, YO, K1; rep from * to last 3 sts, YO, K1, YO, K2.

Rows 2, 4, and 6 (WS): K3, YO, K1, purl to last 4 sts, K1, YO, K3.

Row 3: K2, YO, K1, YO, K3, *K1, YO, cdd, YO, K1; rep from * to last 6 sts, K3, YO, K1, YO, K2.

Row 5: K2, (YO, K1) twice, *K1, YO, cdd, YO, K1; rep from * to last 4 sts, (K1, YO) twice, K2.

Row 7: K2, YO, K1, YO, knit to last 3 sts, YO, K1, YO, K2.

Row 8: K3, YO, knit to last 3 sts, YO, K3.

Rows 9 and 10: Rep rows 7 and 8.

Rep rows 1–10 for patt.

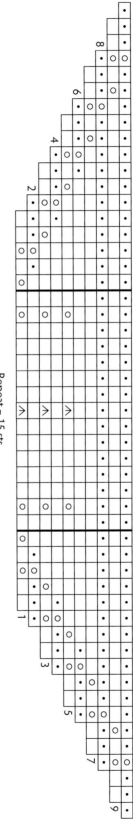

Moyashi Chart A

Repeat = 15 sts

Moyashi Chart B

Repeat = 5 sts

Chart Legend

☐ K on RS, P on WS	○ YO
• P on RS, K on WS	⋏ Cdd

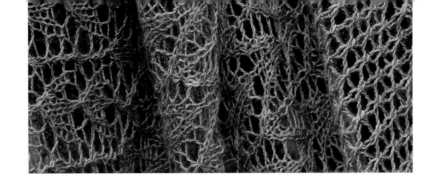

Delicado

designed by the author and knit by Jenni Lesniak

Skill Level: Intermediate

SHAPE: Crescent ⌣

Finished Measurements:
84" × 20"

I love lace-weight shawls, but for years my huge stash of sock yarn kept me from knitting them. Finally, the time came for a beautiful lace-weight shawl. Simple stitch patterns look so much more intricate when knit with a dainty yarn.

FEATURED YARN

2 skeins of Baby Silkpaca from Malabrigo (70% baby alpaca/20% silk; 50 g; 420 yds) in color 866 Arco Iris

MATERIALS

800 yards of lace-weight yarn (0)
US size 4 (3.50 mm) circular needle, 24" or longer, or size required for gauge
Tapestry needle
Blocking supplies

GAUGE

24 sts and 32 rows = 4" in St st

Gauge is not critical for this pattern, but a different gauge will affect yardage and size of shawl.

PATTERN NOTES

Charts are on pages 38 and 39. If you prefer to follow written instructions for the charted material, see "Written Instructions for Charts" on page 36.

If you are using stitch markers to mark each lace repeat on the charts, you'll need to rearrange your stitch markers on rows 3 and 7 of Chart A and row 3 of Chart C.

INSTRUCTIONS

Work garter tab CO (page 93) as foll: CO 2 sts. Knit 10 rows. Turn work 90° and pick up 5 sts along the edge. Turn work 90° and pick up 2 sts from CO edge—9 sts total.

Set-up row (WS): (K3, YO) twice, K3—11 sts.

Work Chart A 5 times—131 sts. Work rows 1–4 of Chart A once more—143 sts.

Work Chart B 9 times—431 sts.

Work Chart C 5 times—591 sts. Work rows 1–3 of Chart C once more—603 sts.

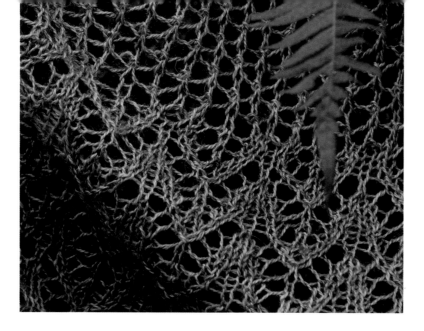

The delicate lace flows seamlessly from one stitch pattern to the next. ◀

STITCH-COUNT BREAKDOWN

First rep of Chart A	35 sts	Sixth rep of Chart B	335 sts
Second rep of Chart A	59 sts	Seventh rep of Chart B	367 sts
Third rep of Chart A	83 sts	Eighth rep of Chart B	399 sts
Fourth rep of Chart A	107 sts	Ninth rep of Chart B	431 sts
Fifth rep of Chart A	131 sts	First rep of Chart C	463 sts
Rows 1–4 only of Chart A	143 sts	Second rep of Chart C	495 sts
First rep of Chart B	175 sts	Third rep of Chart C	527 sts
Second rep of Chart B	207 sts	Fourth rep of Chart C	559 sts
Third rep of Chart B	239 sts	Fifth rep of Chart C	591 sts
Fourth rep of Chart B	271 sts	Rows 1–3 only of Chart C	603 sts
Fifth rep of Chart B	303 sts		

Make It Your Own!

You can repeat Charts B or C or both as many times as you like. Note that changing the number of times you repeat the charts will affect the yardage requirement.

FINISHING

BO loosely knitwise (page 94) on WS. Block shawl to finished measurements given at beg of patt. With tapestry needle, weave in ends.

WRITTEN INSTRUCTIONS FOR CHARTS

If you prefer to follow written instructions rather than a chart, use the row-by-row instructions below.

Chart A

Row 1 (RS): K2, (YO, K1) twice, *YO, sk2p, YO, K1; rep from * to last 3 sts, YO, K1, YO, K2.

Row 2 and all even-numbered rows (WS): K3, YO, K1, purl to last 4 sts, K1, YO, K3.

Row 3: K2, YO, K1, YO, K2, YO, sk2p, *YO, K1, YO, sk2p; rep from * to last 5 sts, YO, K2, YO, K1, YO, K2.

Row 5: K2, YO, K1, YO, K3, *YO, sk2p, YO, K1; rep from * to last 5 sts, K2, YO, K1, YO, K2.

Row 7: K2, YO, K1, YO, K4, YO, sk2p, *YO, K1, YO, sk2p; rep from * to last 7 sts, YO, K4, YO, K1, YO, K2.

Row 8: K3, YO, K1, purl to last 4 sts, K1, YO, K3.

Rep rows 1–8 for patt.

Chart B

Row 1 (RS): K2, (YO, K1) twice, *ssk, (K1, YO) twice, K1, K2tog, K1; rep from * to last 3 sts, YO, K1, YO, K2.

Row 2 and all even-numbered rows (WS): K3, YO, K1, purl to last 4 sts, K1, YO, K3.

Row 3: K2, YO, K1, YO, K4, *ssk, (K1, YO) twice, K1, K2tog, K1; rep from * to last 6 sts, K3, YO, K1, YO, K2.

Row 5: K2, YO, K1, YO, K4, K2tog, YO, K1, *YO, ssk, K3, K2tog, YO, K1; rep from * to last 9 sts, YO, ssk, K4, YO, K1, YO, K2.

Row 7: K2, YO, K1, YO, K2, *K1, YO, ssk, K1, K2tog, YO, K2; rep from * to last 4 sts, (K1, YO) twice, K2.

Row 9: K2, YO, K1, YO, K2, YO, K3, *K2, YO, sk2p, YO, K3; rep from * to last 7 sts, (K2, YO) twice, K1, YO, K2.

Row 10: K3, YO, K1, purl to last 4 sts, K1, YO, K3.

Rep rows 1–10 for patt.

Chart C

Row 1 (RS): K2, (YO, K1) twice, *K2tog, YO, K3, YO, ssk, K1; rep from * to last 3 sts, YO, K1, YO, K2.

Row 2 and all even-numbered rows (WS): K3, (YO, K1) twice, purl to last 5 sts, (K1, YO) twice, K3.

Row 3: K2, YO, K1, YO, K3, YO, sk2p, *YO, K1, YO, sk2p; rep from * to last 6 sts, YO, K3, YO, K1, YO, K2.

Row 5: K2, (YO, K1) twice, *K2, YO, sk2p, YO, K3; rep from * to last 3 sts, YO, K1, YO, K2.

Row 7: K2, YO, K1, YO, K5, *K2, YO, sk2p, YO, K3; rep from * to last 7 sts, K4, YO, K1, YO, K2.

Row 8: K3, (YO, K1) twice, purl to last 5 sts, (K1, YO) twice, K3.

Rep rows 1–8 for patt.

Delicado Chart A

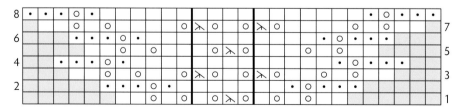

Repeat = 4 sts

Chart Legend

☐ K on RS, P on WS   ⟍ Sk2p

• P on RS, K on WS   ☐ No stitch

○ YO

Top-Down Shawls

Delicado Chart B

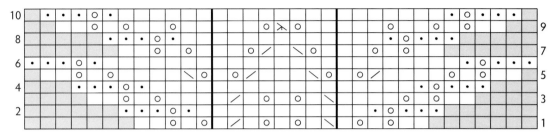

Repeat = 8 sts

Chart Legend

☐	K on RS, P on WS	◲	Ssk
•	P on RS, K on WS	☒	Sk2p
○	YO	▨	No stitch
╱	K2tog		

Delicado Chart C

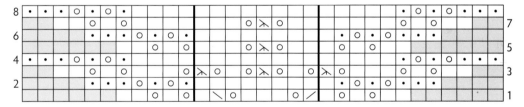

Repeat = 8 sts

Chart Legend

☐	K on RS, P on WS	◲	Ssk
•	P on RS, K on WS	☒	Sk2p
○	YO	▨	No stitch
╱	K2tog		

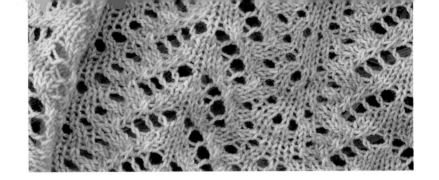

Digitalis

designed by the author and knit by Jenni Lesniak

Skill Level: Experienced

SHAPE: Crescent ⌣

Finished Measurements:
80" × 17"

An interesting take on feather-and-fan makes this shawl a fun and slightly challenging knit. The leaf-lace detail at the edge of the shawl flows beautifully from the body. What a perfect spring shawl!

FEATURED YARN

2 skeins of Hawthorne from Knit Picks (80% superwash fine highland wool/20% nylon; 100 g; 357 yds) in color Wisp

MATERIALS

700 yards of fingering-weight yarn (1)
US size 6 (4.00 mm) circular needle, 24" or longer, or size required for gauge
Tapestry needle
Blocking supplies

GAUGE

16 sts and 28 rows = 4" in St st

Gauge is not critical for this pattern, but a different gauge will affect yardage and size of shawl.

PATTERN NOTES

Charts are on pages 44 and 45. If you prefer to follow written instructions for the charted material, see "Written Instructions for Charts" on page 42.

If you are using stitch markers to mark each 20-stitch lace repeat on the charts, you'll need to rearrange your stitch markers on rows 3, 5, 7, 9, 11, 13, and 15 of Chart C.

INSTRUCTIONS

Work garter tab CO (page 93) as foll: CO 2 sts. Knit 10 rows. Turn work 90° and pick up 5 sts along the edge. Turn work 90° and pick up 2 sts from CO edge—9 sts total.

Set-up row (WS): K3, (YO, K1) 3 times, YO, K3—13 sts.

Work Chart A—29 sts.

Work Chart B 8 times—349 sts.

Work Chart C—389 sts.

By using central double ▶
decreases in this stitch
pattern, the feather-and-fan
effect is much more
dramatic and creates a
deeper chevron within the
lace than more traditional
versions of this stitch.

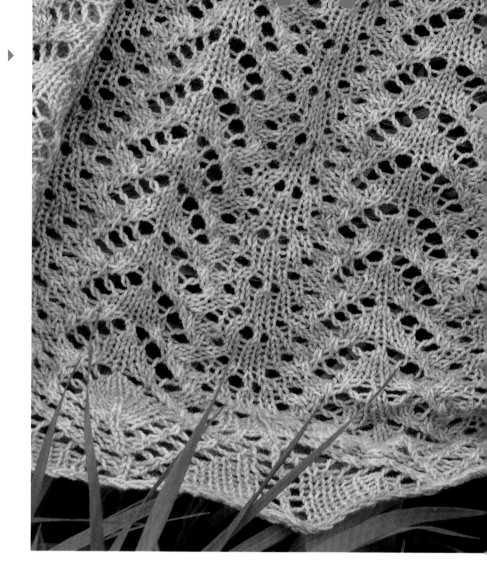

STITCH-COUNT BREAKDOWN	
Chart A	29 sts
First rep of Chart B	69 sts
Second rep of Chart B	109 sts
Third rep of Chart B	149 sts
Fourth rep of Chart B	189 sts
Fifth rep of Chart B	229 sts
Sixth rep of Chart B	269 sts
Seventh rep of Chart B	309 sts
Eighth rep of Chart B	349 sts
Chart C	389 sts

Make It Your Own!

You can repeat Charts B or C or both as many times as you like. Note that changing the number of times you repeat the charts will affect the yardage requirement.

FINISHING

BO loosely knitwise (page 94) on RS. Block shawl to finished measurements given at beg of patt. With tapestry needle, weave in ends.

WRITTEN INSTRUCTIONS FOR CHARTS

If you prefer to follow written instructions rather than a chart, use the row-by-row instructions that follow.

Top-Down Shawls

Row 5: K2, YO, K1, YO, K2, ssk, K2, YO, K2, *K1, YO, K3, cdd, YO, K5, YO, cdd, K3, YO, K2; rep from * to last 10 sts, K1, YO, K2, K2tog, K2, YO, K1, YO, K2.

Row 7: K2, YO, K1, YO, K5, ssk, K3, YO, K1, *YO, K3, cdd, YO, K7, YO, cdd, K3, YO, K1; rep from * to last 13 sts, YO, K3, K2tog, K5, YO, K1, YO, K2.

Row 9: K2, YO, K2, K2tog, YO, K1, YO, cdd, K3, YO, K4, *K3, YO, K3, cdd, YO, K1, YO, cdd, K3, YO, K4; rep from * to last 16 sts, K3, YO, K3, cdd, YO, K1, YO, ssk, K2, YO, K2.

Row 11: K2, YO, K3, K2tog, YO, K3, YO, cdd, K3, YO, K3, *K2, YO, K3, cdd, YO, K3, YO, cdd, K3, YO, K3; rep from * to last 18 sts, K2, YO, K3, cdd, YO, K3, YO, ssk, K3, YO, K2.

Row 13: K2, YO, K4, K2tog, YO, K5, YO, cdd, K3, YO, K2, *K1, YO, K3, cdd, YO, K5, YO, cdd, K3, YO, K2; rep from * to last 20 sts, K1, YO, K3, cdd, YO, K5, YO, ssk, K4, YO, K2.

Row 15: K2, YO, K5, K2tog, YO, K7, YO, cdd, K3, YO, K1, *YO, K3, cdd, YO, K7, YO, cdd, K3, YO, K1; rep from * to last 22 sts, YO, K3, cdd, YO, K7, YO, ssk, K5, YO, K2.

Row 16: K3, YO, K1, purl to last 4 sts, K1, YO, K3.

Rep rows 1–16 for patt.

Chart A

Row 1 (RS): K2, YO, K1, YO, K7, YO, K1, YO, K2.

Rows 2 and 4 (WS): K3, YO, K1, purl to last 4 sts, K1, YO, K3.

Row 3: K2, YO, K1, YO, K2, K2tog, YO, K5, YO, ssk, K2, YO, K1, YO, K2.

Row 5: K2, YO, K5, K2tog, YO, K7, YO, ssk, K5, YO, K2.

Row 6: K3, YO, K1, purl to last 4 sts, K1, YO, K3.

Chart B

Row 1 (RS): K2, YO, K1, YO, K2, *K3, YO, K3, cdd, YO, K1, YO, cdd, K3, YO, K4; rep from * to last 4 sts, (K1, YO) twice, K2.

Row 2 and all even-numbered rows (WS): K3, YO, K1, purl to last 4 sts, K1, YO, K3.

Row 3: K2, YO, K1, YO, K5, *K2, YO, K3, cdd, YO, K3, YO, cdd, K3, YO, K3; rep from * to last 7 sts, K4, YO, K1, YO, K2.

Chart C

Row 1 (RS): K2, YO, K1, YO, K2, *K1, (YO, ssk) twice, YO, K3, cdd, K3, (YO, K2tog) twice, YO, K2; rep from * to last 4 sts, (K1, YO) twice, K2.

Row 2 and all even-numbered rows (WS): K3, YO, K1, purl to last 4 sts, K1, YO, K3.

Row 3: K2, YO, K1, YO, K3, YO, cdd, *YO, K1, (YO, ssk) twice, YO, K2, cdd, K2, (YO, K2tog) twice, YO, K1, YO, cdd; rep from * to last 6 sts, YO, K3, YO, K1, YO, K2.

Row 5: K2, YO, K1, YO, K2, K2tog, YO, K2, YO, cdd, *YO, K2, (YO, ssk) twice, YO, K1, cdd, K1, (YO, K2tog) twice, YO, K2, YO, cdd; rep from * to last 9 sts, YO, K2, YO, ssk, K2, YO, K1, YO, K2.

Row 7: K2, YO, K1, YO, K2, (K2tog, YO) twice, K3, YO, cdd, *YO, K3, (YO, ssk) twice, YO, cdd, (YO, K2tog) twice, YO, K3, YO, cdd; rep from * to last 12 sts, YO, K3, (YO, ssk) twice, K2, YO, K1, YO, K2.

Row 9: K2, YO, K5, (K2tog, YO) twice, K4, YO, cdd, *YO, K4, YO, ssk, YO, K1, cdd, K1, YO, K2tog, YO, K4, YO, cdd; rep from * to last 15 sts, YO, K4, (YO, ssk) twice, K5, YO, K2.

Row 11: K2, YO, K3, YO, ssk, YO, cdd, YO, K2tog, YO, K5, YO, cdd, *YO, K5, YO, ssk, YO, cdd, YO, K2tog, YO, K5, YO, cdd; rep from * to last 17 sts, YO, K5, YO, ssk, YO, cdd, YO, K2tog, YO, K3, YO, K2.

Row 13: K2, YO, K6, YO, K1, cdd, K1, YO, K6, YO, cdd, *YO, K6, YO, K1, cdd, K1, YO, K6, YO, cdd; rep from * to last 19 sts, YO, K6, YO, K1, cdd, K1, YO, K6, YO, K2.

Row 15: K2, YO, K9, YO, cdd, *YO, K7, YO, cdd; rep from * to last 11 sts, YO, K9, YO, K2.

Row 16: K3, YO, K1, purl to last 4 sts, K1, YO, K3.

Rep rows 1–16 for patt.

Digitalis Chart A

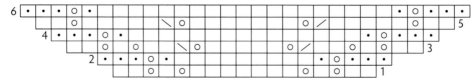

Chart Legend

☐ K on RS, P on WS	╱ K2tog
⊡ P on RS, K on WS	╲ Ssk
⊙ YO	

Top-Down Shawls

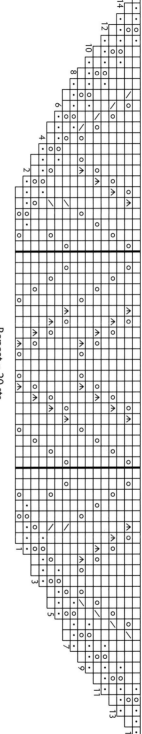

Digitalis Chart B

Repeat = 20 sts

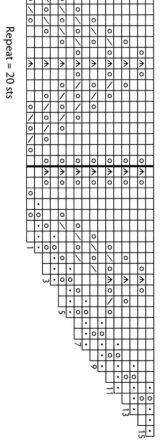

Digitalis Chart C

Repeat = 20 sts

Chart Legend

	K on RS, P on WS		K2tog
•	P on RS, K on WS	/	Ssk
o	YO	⋏	Cdd

Fiddleheads

designed by the author and knit by Melissa Rusk

Skill Level: Intermediate

SHAPE: Crescent ⌣

Finished Measurements:
84"×14"

This shawl is my love letter to garter stitch and lace, a combination that is my absolute favorite to design. The simple garter-stitch details in the lace pattern at the edge of this shawl make me fall in love with the garter and lace all over again.

FEATURED YARN

2 skeins of Cashluxe Fine from SweetGeorgia Yarns (70% superwash merino/20% cashmere/10% nylon; 115 g; 400 yds) in color Fern

MATERIALS

750 yards of fingering-weight yarn 🄵
US size 5 (3.75 mm) circular needle, 24" or longer, or size required for gauge
Tapestry needle
Blocking supplies

GAUGE

20 sts and 28 rows = 4" in St st

Gauge is not critical for this pattern, but a different gauge will affect yardage and size of shawl.

PATTERN NOTES

Chart is on page 49. If you prefer to follow written instructions for the charted material, see "Written Instructions for Chart" on page 48.

The body of the shawl is worked in garter stitch. You may find it helpful to use a locking stitch marker to mark the right side of your work.

INSTRUCTIONS

Work garter tab CO (page 93) as foll: CO 2 sts. Knit 16 rows. Turn work 90° and pick up 8 sts along the edge. Turn work 90° and pick up 2 sts from CO edge—12 sts total.

Set-up row (WS): K3, (YO, K1) to the last 3 sts, YO, K3—19 sts.

Row 1 (RS): K2, YO, K1, YO, knit to last 3 sts, YO, K1, YO, K2—4 sts inc, 23 sts total.

Row 2: K3, YO, knit to last 3 sts, YO, K3—2 sts inc, 25 sts total.

Rep rows 1 and 2 another 31 times—211 sts.

Work chart 4 times—403 sts.

Work rows 1–13 of chart once more—449 sts.

Make It Your Own!

Since you only have one chart to work for this shawl, it's easy to customize. Repeat the chart as many times as you like. Note that changing the number of times you repeat the chart will affect the yardage requirement.

STITCH-COUNT BREAKDOWN	
First rep of Chart	259 sts
Second rep of Chart	307 sts
Third rep of Chart	355 sts
Fourth rep of Chart	403 sts
Rows 1–13 of Chart	449 sts

FINISHING

BO loosely knitwise (page 94) on WS. Block shawl to finished measurements given at beg of patt. With tapestry needle, weave in ends.

WRITTEN INSTRUCTIONS FOR CHART

If you prefer to follow written instructions rather than a chart, use the row-by-row instructions below.

Row 1 (RS): K2, (YO, K1) twice, *YO, K4, cdd, K4, YO, K1; rep from * to last 3 sts, YO, K1, YO, K2.

Row 2 and all even-numbered rows (WS): K3, YO, K1, purl to last 4 sts, K1, YO, K3.

Row 3: K2, YO, K1, YO, K4, *K1, YO, K3, cdd, K3, YO, K2tog, YO; rep from * to last 6 sts, K3, YO, K1, YO, K2.

Row 5: K2, YO, K1, YO, K2, (K2tog, YO) twice, K1, *YO, ssk, YO, K2, cdd, K2, YO, K2tog, YO, K1; rep from * to

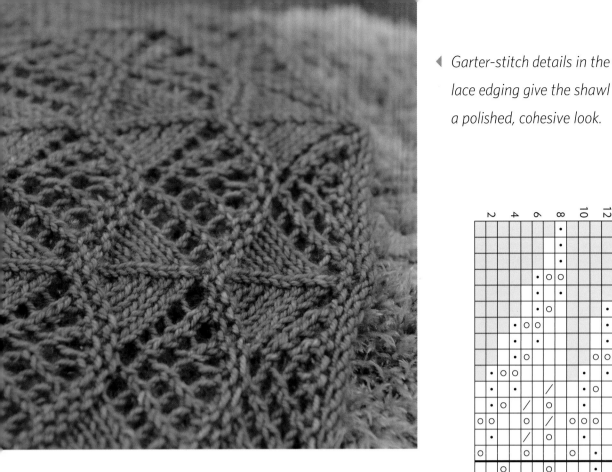

 *Garter-stitch details in the lace edging give the shawl a polished, cohesive look.*

last 9 sts, (YO, ssk) twice, K2, YO, K1, YO, K2.

Row 7: K2, YO, K1, YO, K4, (K2tog, YO) 3 times, *K1, YO, ssk, YO, K1, cdd, K1, (YO, K2tog) twice, YO; rep from * to last 12 sts, K1, (YO, ssk) twice, K4, YO, K1, YO, K2.

Row 9: K2, (YO, K1) twice, *(YO, ssk) twice, YO, cdd, (YO, K2tog) twice, YO, K1; rep from * to last 3 sts, YO, K1, YO, K2.

Row 11: K2, (YO, K1) 3 times, purl to last 5 sts, (K1, YO) 3 times, K2.

Row 13: K2, (YO, K1) 4 times, purl to last 6 sts, (K1, YO) 4 times, K2.

Row 14: K3, YO, K1, purl to last 4 sts, K1, YO, K3.

Rep rows 1–14 for patt.

Chart Legend

☐ K on RS, P on WS	◻ Ssk
• P on RS, K on WS	⋏ Cdd
○ YO	No stitch (shaded)
◹ K2tog	

Fiddleheads Chart

Repeat = 12 sts

Struttura

designed by the author and knit by Jenni Lesniak

Skill Level: Intermediate

SHAPE: Half-Circle ⌣

Finished Measurements: 52" × 18"

As much as I love a lace shawl, sometimes it's nice to bring texture into the mix. The Stitch Sprouts Yellowstone yarn used in Struttura is perfect for highlighting the textured stitch patterns. Those purl stitches really pop!

FEATURED YARN

2 skeins of Yellowstone from Stitch Sprouts (80% merino/20% silk; 100 g; 285 yds) in color Steamboat Geyser

MATERIALS

550 yards of sport-weight yarn 🧶**2**
US size 6 (4.00 mm) circular needle, 24" or longer, or size required for gauge
Tapestry needle
Blocking supplies

GAUGE

20 sts and 28 rows = 4" in garter st

Gauge is not critical for this pattern, but a different gauge will affect yardage and size of shawl.

PATTERN NOTES

Charts are on page 53. If you prefer to follow written instructions for the charted material, see "Written Instructions for Charts" on page 52.

This shawl is worked primarily in knits and purls, creating a texture that may make it difficult to distinguish the right side and wrong side of the piece. You may find it helpful to use a locking stitch marker to mark the right side of your work.

INSTRUCTIONS

Work garter tab CO (page 93) as foll: CO 3 sts. Knit 20 rows. Turn work 90° and pick up 10 sts along the edge. Turn work 90° and pick up 3 sts from CO edge—16 sts total.

Set-up row (WS): Knit all sts.

Inc row (RS): K3, (YO, K1) to the last 3 sts, K3—26 sts.

Knit 3 rows.

Work inc row—46 sts.

Knit 7 rows.

Work inc row—86 sts.

Mirror-image stitch patterns ▶ *are worked in the body of the shawl to create dimension and interest.*

Next row: Knit all sts.

Work Chart A twice (20 rows).

Work inc row—166 sts.

Next row: Knit all sts.

Work Chart B 4 times (40 rows).

Work inc row—326 sts.

Next row: Knit all sts.

Work Chart C 5 times (50 rows).

Work rows 1–9 of Chart C once more.

Next row (WS): Knit all sts.

Make It Your Own!

You can repeat Chart C as many times as you like, up to 8 times. Then work rows 1–9 of Chart C and a final row on the wrong side, knitting all stitches once more before binding off. Note that changing the number of times you repeat the chart will affect the yardage requirement.

FINISHING

BO loosely knitwise (page 94) on RS. Block shawl to finished measurements given at beg of patt. With tapestry needle, weave in ends.

WRITTEN INSTRUCTIONS FOR CHARTS

If you prefer to follow written instructions rather than a chart, use the row-by-row instructions below.

Chart A

Row 1 and all odd-numbered rows (RS): Knit all sts.

Row 2 (WS): K3, *K1, P4; rep from * to last 3 sts, K3.

Row 4: K3, *K2, P3; rep from * to last 3 sts, K3.

Row 6: K3, *K3, P2; rep from * to last 3 sts, K3.

Row 8: K3, *K4, P1; rep from * to last 3 sts, K3.

Row 10: Knit all sts.

Rep rows 1–10 for patt.

Chart B

Row 1 and all odd-numbered rows (RS): Knit all sts.

Row 2 (WS): K3, *P4, K1; rep from * to last 3 sts, K3.

Row 4: K3, *P3, K2; rep from * to last 3 sts, K3.

Row 6: K3, *P2, K3; rep from * to last 3 sts, K3.

◀ *You can have a lovely edge to your shawl even without lace!*

Stuttura Chart A

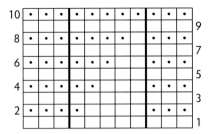

Repeat = 5 sts

Stuttura Chart B

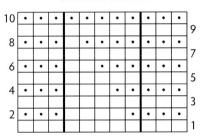

Repeat = 5 sts

Row 8: K3, *P1, K4; rep from * to last 3 sts, K3.

Row 10: Knit all sts.

Rep rows 1–10 for patt.

Chart C

Row 1 and all odd-numbered rows (RS): Knit all sts.

Row 2 (WS): K3, *P4, K2, P4; rep from * to last 3 sts, K3.

Row 4: K3, *P3, K4, P3; rep from * to last 3 sts, K3.

Row 6: K3, *(P2, K2) twice, P2; rep from * to last 3 sts, K3.

Row 8: K3, *P1, K2, P4, K2, P1; rep from * to last 3 sts, K3.

Row 10: K3, *K2, P6, K2; rep from * to last 3 sts, K3.

Rep rows 1–10 for patt.

Stuttura Chart C

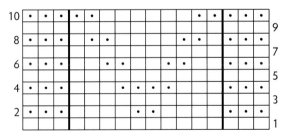

Repeat = 10 sts

Chart Legend

☐ K on RS, P on WS   ⊡ P on RS, K on WS

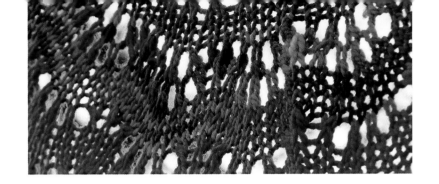

Barthlott

designed by the author and knit by Melissa Rusk

Skill Level: Intermediate

SHAPE: Half-Circle ⬭

**Finished Measurements:
50" × 16"**

Simple lace patterns are all you need on this beautiful shawl; the innovative yarn does all the work. Barthlott is worked with one ball of yarn, but I think a huge half-circle shawl using two balls would be absolutely stunning.

FEATURED YARN

1 ball of Frolicking Feet Transitions from Done Roving Yarns (100% superwash merino, 113 g; 480 yds) in color 24 Easter Cactus

MATERIALS

480 yards of fingering-weight yarn 🧶**1**
US size 5 (3.75 mm) circular needle, 24" or longer, or size required for gauge
Tapestry needle
Blocking supplies

GAUGE

20 sts and 28 rows = 4" in St st

Gauge is not critical for this pattern, but a different gauge will affect yardage and size of shawl.

PATTERN NOTES

Charts are on page 57. If you prefer to follow written instructions for the charted material, see "Written Instructions for Charts" on page 56.

INSTRUCTIONS

Work garter tab CO (page 93) as foll: CO 3 sts. Knit 22 rows. Turn work 90° and pick up 11 sts along the edge. Turn work 90° and pick up 3 sts from CO edge—17 sts total.

Set-up row (WS): Knit all sts.

Inc row (RS): K3, (K1, YO) to the last 4 sts, K4—27 sts.

Row 2: K3, purl to last 3 sts, K3.

Row 3: Knit all sts.

Row 4: Rep row 2.

Work inc row—47 sts.

Next row: K3, purl to last 3 sts, K3.

Work Chart A once (6 rows).

Work inc row—87 sts.

Next row: K3, purl to last 3 sts, K3.

Work Chart A twice (12 rows).

Work inc row—167 sts.

The slight waves created in the stitch pattern show off this interesting yarn beautifully! ▶

Next row: K3, purl to last 3 sts, K3.

Work Chart A 5 times (30 rows).

Work inc row—327 sts.

Next row: K3, purl to last 3 sts, K3.

Work Chart B 8 times (48 rows).

FINISHING

BO loosely knitwise (page 94) on RS. Block shawl to finished measurements given at beg of patt. With tapestry needle, weave in ends.

Make It Bigger!

You can repeat Chart B an additional 3 times. To make the shawl even bigger, work the increase row again— 647 sts, then work the next row as K3, purl to last 3 sts, K3. You can then work either chart to desired length, up to 132 rows total. That's one big shawl! Note that adding repeats will affect the yardage required.

WRITTEN INSTRUCTIONS FOR CHARTS

If you prefer to follow written instructions rather than a chart, use the row-by-row instructions below.

Chart A

Row 1 (RS): K4, *YO, K1, YO, ssk, cdd, K2tog, (YO, K1) twice; rep from * to last 3 sts, K3.

Row 2 (WS): K3, purl to last 3 sts, K3.

Rows 3 and 5: Knit all sts.

Rows 4 and 6: Rep row 2.

Rep rows 1–6 for patt.

Chart B

Row 1 (RS): K4, *YO, K1, YO, ssk, cdd, K2tog, (YO, K1) twice; rep from * to last 3 sts, K3.

Row 2 (WS): Knit all sts.

Rows 3 and 4: Rep rows 1 and 2.

Rows 5 and 6: Knit all sts.

Rep rows 1–6 for patt.

Barthlott Chart A

Repeat = 10 sts

Barthlott Chart B

Repeat = 10 sts

Chart Legend

☐ K on RS, P on WS		╱ K2tog	
• P on RS, K on WS		╲ Ssk	
○ YO		⋏ Cdd	

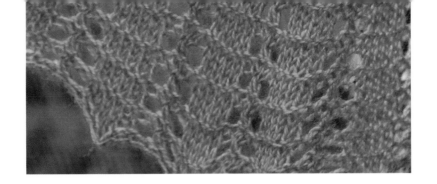

Spiranthes

designed by the author and knit by Jenni Lesniak

Skill Level: Intermediate

SHAPE: Half-Circle ▽

Finished Measurements:
44" × 14"

Give me some sock yarn and stitch patterns with touches of garter stitch, and you know I'm happy. The Spiranthes shawl is heaven on earth for me: soothing, easy stitches with a hint of garter stitch and lace make it a breeze to knit.

FEATURED YARN

1 skein of Diva from Leading Men Fiber Arts (80% superwash merino/20% silk; 150 g; 600 yds) in color Saffron

MATERIALS

530 yards of fingering-weight yarn (**1**)
US size 5 (3.75 mm) circular needle, 24" or longer, or size required for gauge
Tapestry needle
Blocking supplies

GAUGE

22 sts and 28 rows = 4" in St st

Gauge is not critical for this pattern, but a different gauge will affect yardage and size of shawl.

PATTERN NOTES

Charts are on page 61. If you prefer to follow written instructions for the charted material, see "Written Instructions for Charts" on page 61.

INSTRUCTIONS

Work garter tab CO (page 93) as foll: CO 3 sts. Knit 20 rows. Turn work 90° and pick up 10 sts along the edge. Turn work 90° and pick up 3 sts from CO edge—16 sts total.

Set-up row (WS): K3, purl to last 3 sts, K3.

Inc row (RS): K6, (YO, K1) to last 5 sts, K5—21 sts.

Row 2: K3, purl to last 3 sts, K3.

Work inc row—31 sts.

Next row: Rep row 2.

Next row: Knit all sts.

Next row: Rep row 2.

Work inc row—51 sts.

Next row: Rep row 2.

Work Chart A once (6 rows).

Work inc row—91 sts.

Next row: Rep row 2.

Work Chart B once (12 rows).

Work inc row—171 sts.

◀ A vertical stitch pattern used at the edging of this shawl makes it a little fun—and a little funky too.

Next row: Rep row 2.

Work Chart B twice (24 rows).

Work inc row—331 sts.

Next row: Rep row 2.

Work Chart C 12 times (48 rows).

Make It Bigger!

If you'd like to make your shawl even bigger, work the increase row again—651 sts, and work the next row as K3, purl to last 3 sts, K3. You can then work either Chart B or Chart C to desired length, up to 96 rows total. Note that changing the number of times you repeat the charts will affect the yardage requirement.

FINISHING

BO loosely knitwise (page 94) on RS. Block shawl to finished measurements given at beg of patt. With tapestry needle, weave in ends.

Top-Down Shawls

WRITTEN INSTRUCTIONS FOR CHARTS

If you prefer to follow written instructions rather than a chart, use the row-by-row instructions below.

Chart A

Row 1 (RS): Knit all sts.

Row 2 (WS): K3, purl to last 3 sts, K3.

Row 3: K3, *K5, P3; rep from * to the last 8 sts, K8.

Row 4: *K3, P5; rep from * to the last 3 sts, K3.

Row 5: K3, *K5, YO, cdd, YO; rep from * to the last 8 sts, K8.

Row 6: Rep row 2.

Chart B

Row 1 (RS): Knit all sts.

Row 2 (WS): K3, purl to last 3 sts, K3.

Row 3: K3, *K1, P3, K4; rep from * to end.

Row 4: (K3, P1) twice, *P4, K3, P1; rep from * to last 3 sts, K3.

Row 5: K3, *K1, YO, cdd, YO, K4; rep from * to end.

Row 6: Rep row 2.

Row 7: Rep row 1.

Row 8: Rep row 2.

Row 9: K3, *K5, P3; rep from * to last 8 sts, K8.

Row 10: *K3, P5; rep from * to last 3 sts, K3.

Row 11: K3, *K5, YO, cdd, YO; rep from * to last 8 sts, K8.

Row 12: Rep row 2.

Rep rows 1–12 for patt.

Chart C

Row 1 (RS): Knit all sts.

Row 2 (WS): K3, purl to last 3 sts, K3.

Row 3: K3, *K1, YO, cdd, YO, K4; rep from * to end.

Row 4: Knit all sts.

Rep rows 1–4 for patt.

Spiranthes Chart A

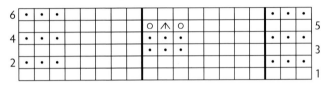

Repeat = 8 sts

Spiranthes Chart B

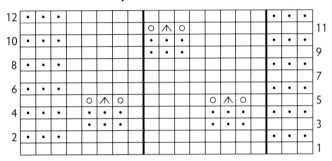

Repeat = 8 sts

Spiranthes Chart C

Repeat = 8 sts

Chart Legend

☐ K on RS, P on WS   ⊙ YO

• P on RS, K on WS   ⋀ Cdd

Nymans

designed by the author and knit by Cathy Rusk

Skill Level: Intermediate

SHAPE: Half-Circle ▢

**Finished Measurements:
52"×18"**

Large leaf-lace stitch patterns are geometric and delicate at the same time, which makes me gravitate toward them. The Nymans shawl combines a traditional leaf-lace pattern with a textured geometric pattern to create a truly unique shawl.

FEATURED YARN

4 skeins of Superwash DK from SweetGeorgia Yarns (100% superwash merino, 115 g; 256 yds) in color Wisteria

MATERIALS

850 yards of DK-weight yarn ((**3**))
US size 7 (4.50 mm) circular needle, 24" or longer, or size required for gauge
Tapestry needle
Blocking supplies

GAUGE

16 sts and 28 rows = 4" in St st

Gauge is not critical for this pattern, but a different gauge will affect yardage and size of shawl.

PATTERN NOTES

Charts are on page 66. If you prefer to follow written instructions for the charted material, see "Written Instructions for Charts" on page 65.

INSTRUCTIONS

Work garter tab CO (page 93) as foll: CO 3 sts. Knit 38 rows. Turn work 90° and pick up 19 sts along the edge. Turn work 90° and pick up 3 sts from CO edge—25 sts total.

Section 1

Set-up row (WS): Knit all sts.

Inc row (RS): K3, (K1, YO) to the last 4 sts, K4—43 sts.

Row 2 (WS): K3, purl to last 3 sts, K3.

Row 3: Knit all sts.

Row 4: Rep row 2.

Section 2

Work inc row—79 sts.

Row 2 (WS): K3, purl to last 3 sts, K3.

Row 3: Knit all sts.

Row 4: Rep row 2.

Rows 5–8: Rep rows 3 and 4 twice.

Section 3

Work inc row—151 sts.

Next row: K3, purl to last 3 sts, K3.

Work Chart A once (16 rows).

Section 4

Work inc row—295 sts.

Next row: K3, purl to last 3 sts, K3.

Work Chart A twice (32 rows).

Section 5

Work inc row—583 sts.

Next row: K3, purl to last 3 sts, K3.

Work Chart B twice (20 rows).

Work Chart C once (5 rows).

◀ *The triangular stitch pattern along the bottom of the shawl creates a simple but striking edge.*

Make It Bigger!

You can repeat Chart B an additional 4 times before moving on to Chart C. Note that changing the number of times you repeat the chart will affect the yardage requirement.

FINISHING

BO loosely knitwise (page 94) on WS. Block shawl to finished measurements given at beg of patt. With tapestry needle, weave in ends.

WRITTEN INSTRUCTIONS FOR CHARTS

If you prefer to follow written instructions rather than a chart, use the row-by-row instructions below.

Chart A

Row 1 (RS): K4, *YO, K4, ssk, K2tog, YO, K1, YO, ssk, K2tog, K4, YO, K1; rep from * to last 3 sts, K3.

Row 2 and all even-numbered rows (WS): K3, purl to last 3 sts, K3.

Row 3: K4, *YO, K4, K3tog, (K1, YO) twice, K1, sssk, K4, YO, K1; rep from * to last 3 sts, K3.

Row 5: K4, *K4, K2tog, K2, YO, K1, YO, K2, ssk, K5; rep from * to last 3 sts, K3.

Row 7: K4, *K3, K2tog, K3, YO, K1, YO, K3, ssk, K4; rep from * to last 3 sts, K3.

Row 9: K4, *YO, ssk, K2tog, K4, YO, K1, YO, K4, ssk, K2tog, YO, K1; rep from * to last 3 sts, K3.

Row 11: K4, *YO, K1, sssk, K4, YO, K1, YO, K4, K3tog, K1, YO, K1; rep from * to last 3 sts, K3.

Row 13: K4, *YO, K2, ssk, K9, K2tog, K2, YO, K1; rep from * to last 3 sts, K3.

Row 15: K4, *YO, K3, ssk, K7, K2tog, K3, YO, K1; rep from * to last 3 sts, K3.

Row 16: K3, purl to last 3 sts, K3.

Rep rows 1–16 for patt.

Chart B

Row 1 (RS): K4, *YO, K3, ssk, P7, K2tog, K3, YO, K1; rep from * to last 3 sts, K3.

Row 2 and all even-numbered rows (WS): K3, purl to last 3 sts, K3.

Row 3: K4, *K1, YO, K3, ssk, P5, K2tog, K3, YO, K2; rep from * to last 3 sts, K3.

Row 5: K4, *K2, YO, K3, ssk, P3, K2tog, K3, YO, K3; rep from * to last 3 sts, K3.

Row 7: K4, *K3, YO, K3, ssk, P1, K2tog, K3, YO, K4; rep from * to last 3 sts, K3.

Row 9: K4, *K4, YO, K3, sk2p, K3, YO, K5; rep from * to last 3 sts, K3.

Row 10: K3, purl to last 3 sts, K3.

Rep rows 1–10 for patt.

Chart C

Row 1 (RS): K4, *K5, YO, K2, sk2p, K2, YO, K6; rep from * to last 3 sts, K3.

Rows 2 and 4: K3, purl to last 3 sts, K3.

Row 3: K4, *K6, YO, K1, sk2p, K1, YO, K7; rep from * to last 3 sts, K3.

Row 5: K4, *K7, YO, sk2p, YO, K8; rep from * to last 3 sts, K3.

Nymans Chart A

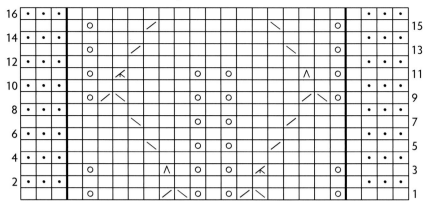

Repeat = 18 sts

Chart Legend

☐	K on RS, P on WS	╲	Ssk
•	P on RS, K on WS	⋀	Sssk
○	YO	⋌	K3tog
╱	K2tog		

Nymans Chart B

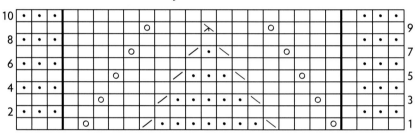

Repeat = 18 sts

Chart Legend

☐	K on RS, P on WS	╱	K2tog
•	P on RS, K on WS	╲	Ssk
○	YO	⋏	Sk2p

Nymans Chart C

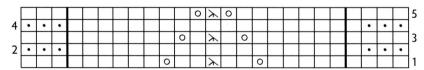

Repeat = 18 sts

Chart Legend

☐	K on RS, P on WS	○	YO
•	P on RS, K on WS	⋏	Sk2p

Design Your Own Shawl

Now the fun really begins—designing your own shawl! In this section you'll find stitch patterns and templates to create your own. Be sure to read the information below about yarn requirements and gauge; you'll find this information helpful, and it will aid you in completing a shawl you're truly in love with. (The shawl featured above is a crescent shawl—Delicado on page 35.)

If you've knit a lot of shawls, you probably have a good idea of what gauge you like and how much yarn you typically use. If you're new to shawl knitting or aren't sure where to start, use the chart below as a guide.

The low end of the yardage listed will make you a small shawlette. If you want to hop on the style (which I love) of a larger shawl, you'll want to use the higher end of that yardage range.

So what about gauge? It's your shawl; you need to find the gauge that makes you happy. Remember, these are lace shawls, so you likely want your gauge to be a little looser than what's recommended on the ball band (to show all the delicate details).

The beauty of the top-down shawl is that it's easy to just knit until you are about to run out of yarn!

RECOMMENDED YARN AND NEEDLES		
YARN WEIGHT	**YARDAGE**	**NEEDLE SIZES**
Fingering	450–800+ yards	US size 4 to US size 6
Sport	350–750+ yards	US size 5 to US size 7
DK	300–700+ yards	US size 6 to US size 8
Worsted	250–700+ yards	US size 7 to US size 9

Wedge Shawls

▽ Top-down wedge shawls are a great place to start. Once your charts are set up, it's easy to keep repeating them until you have the shawl size you want (or you run out of yarn!).

One great thing about the triangle shawl is that you can push it beyond simply making a triangle. The traditional top-down triangle shawl is made up of two smaller triangles that form a larger triangle. But why not take three smaller triangles and work them in a similar manner to make a shawl that's a totally different shape?

In this section you will find two templates: a 2-wedge construction, as used for the Kokedama shawl (page 19) shown above, and a 3-wedge construction. Just plug any of the charts on pages 70–75 into the pattern template of your choice, and create a shawl that is uniquely yours.

2-WEDGE SHAWL TEMPLATE

You'll need 4 stitch markers for this shawl.

Work garter tab CO (page 93) as foll: CO 3 sts. Knit 6 rows. Turn work 90° and pick up 3 sts along the edge. Turn work 90° and pick up 3 sts from CO edge—9 sts total.

Set-Up Rows

Set-up row (WS): K3, P3, K3.

Row 1 (RS): K3, PM, YO, K1, YO, PM, K1 (this is the center st), PM, YO, K1, YO, PM, K3—13 sts.

Row 2 (WS): K3, purl to last 3 sts, K3.

Row 3: K3, SM, YO, knit to next marker, YO, SM, K1, SM, YO, knit to last marker, YO, SM, K3—17 sts.

Work rows 2 and 3 twice more—25 sts. Work row 2 once more.

Body of Shawl

Cont working first 3 and last 3 edge sts in garter st (knit every row) and working the center st in St st (K on RS/P on WS). In between the stitch markers on each half of the shawl, work desired st patt.

Pick a chart! Once you have worked the **full 16 rows of the chart,** you can work a different st patt or work the same one again. It's your shawl—it's up to you!

Rows will be worked as foll for remainder of shawl:

RS: K3, SM, work row of desired st patt to marker, SM, K1, SM, work row of desired st patt once more to marker, SM, K3.

WS: K3, SM, work row of desired st patt to marker, SM, P1, SM, work row of desired st patt once more to marker, SM, K3.

Work shawl to desired length, ending with row 16 of st patt.

Finishing

BO loosely knitwise (page 94) on RS. Block shawl. With tapestry needle, weave in ends.

3-WEDGE SHAWL TEMPLATE

You'll need 6 stitch markers for this shawl.

Work garter tab CO (page 93) as foll: CO 3 sts. Knit 10 rows. Turn work 90° and pick up 5 sts along the edge. Turn work 90° and pick up 3 sts from CO edge—11 sts total.

Set-Up Rows

Set-up row (WS): K3, P5, K3.

Row 1 (RS): K3, [PM, YO, K1, YO, PM, K1 (this is the spine st)] twice, PM, YO, K1, YO, PM, K3—17 sts.

Row 2 (WS): K3, purl to last 3 sts, K3.

Row 3: K3, (SM, YO, knit to next marker, YO, SM, K1) twice, SM, YO, knit to last marker, YO, SM, K3—23 sts.

Work rows 2 and 3 twice more—35 sts. Work row 2 once more.

Body of Shawl

Cont working first 3 and last 3 edge sts in garter st (knit every row) and working the spine sts (the one st separated by stitch markers on either side) in St st (K on RS/P on WS). In between the stitch markers in each of the 3 body sections of the shawl (the sections that start with 9 sts), work desired st patt.

Pick a chart! Once you have worked the **full 16 rows of the chart,** you can work a different chart or work the same one again. It's your shawl—it's up to you!

Make It Your Own!

All the stitch patterns in this section are a multiple of 8 stitches plus 1 and are worked over 16 rows. If you're feeling brave, pick a stitch pattern from a stitch dictionary that is 8 stitches wide and 4, 8, or 16 rows long and make your own chart!

Rows will be worked as foll for remainder of shawl:

RS: K3, (SM, work row of desired st patt to marker, SM, K1) twice, SM, work row of desired st patt to marker, SM, K3.

WS: K3, (SM, work row of desired st patt to marker, SM, P1) twice, SM, work row of desired st patt to marker, SM, K3.

Work shawl to desired length, ending with row 16 of st patt.

Finishing

BO loosely knitwise (page 94) on RS. Block shawl. With tapestry needle, weave in ends.

PATTERN STITCHES FOR WEDGE SHAWL TEMPLATES

Choose any of the stitch patterns on pages 70–75 to create a wedge shawl. Each pattern has a chart, written instructions, and a photo of what the pattern looks like.

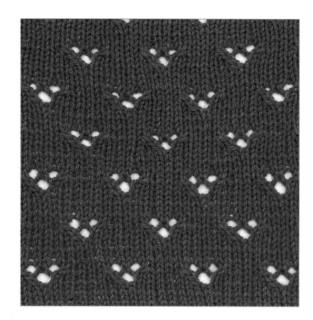

WRITTEN INSTRUCTIONS FOR EYELET CHEVRONS CHART

If you prefer to follow row-by-row instructions rather than a chart, use the instructions below.

Row 1 (RS): YO, knit to marker, YO.

Row 2 and all even-numbered rows (WS): Purl all sts.

Row 3: Rep row 1.

Row 5: YO, K3, *K3, YO, ssk, K3; rep from * to 2 sts before marker, K2, YO.

Row 7: YO, K4, *K1, K2tog, YO, K1, YO, ssk, K2; rep from * to 3 sts before marker, K3, YO.

Row 9: Rep row 1.

Row 11: Rep row 1.

Row 13: YO, K6, YO, *ssk, K6, YO; rep from * to 7 sts before marker, ssk, K5, YO.

Row 15: YO, K5, K2tog, YO, K1, *YO, ssk, K3, K2tog, YO, K1; rep from * to 7 sts before marker, YO, ssk, K5, YO.

Row 16: Purl all sts.

Rep rows 1–16 for patt.

Wedge Shawl Template: Eyelet Chevrons Chart

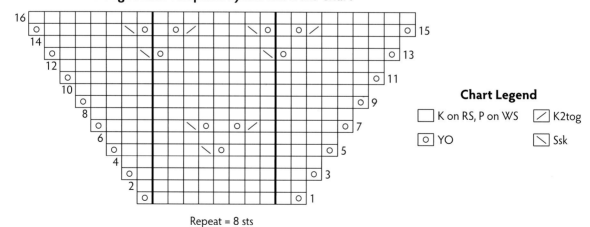

Repeat = 8 sts

Chart Legend

☐ K on RS, P on WS   ╱ K2tog

○ YO   ╲ Ssk

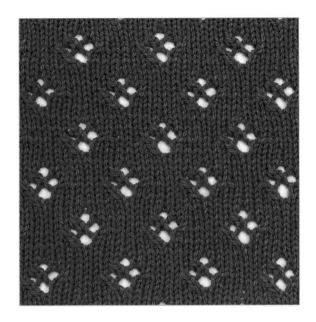

WRITTEN INSTRUCTIONS FOR EYELET MINI-DIAMONDS CHART

If you prefer to follow row-by-row instructions rather than a chart, use the instructions below.

Row 1 (RS): YO, knit to marker, YO.

Row 2 and all even-numbered rows (WS): Purl all sts.

Row 3: YO, K2, *K3, YO, ssk, K3; rep from * to 1 st before marker, K1, YO.

Row 5: YO, K3, *K1, K2tog, YO, K1, YO, ssk, K2; rep from * to 2 sts before marker, K2, YO.

Row 7: YO, K4, *K3, YO, ssk, K3; rep from * to 3 sts before marker, K3, YO.

Row 9: Rep row 1.

Row 11: Rep row 3.

Row 13: Rep row 5.

Row 15: Rep row 7.

Row 16: Purl all sts.

Rep rows 1–16 for patt.

Wedge Shawl Template: Eyelet Mini-Diamonds Chart

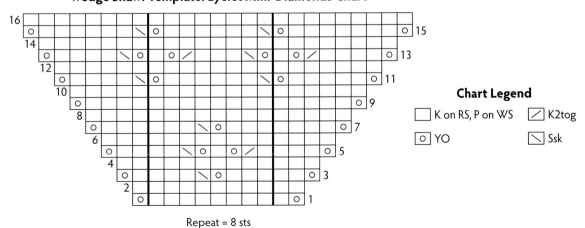

Repeat = 8 sts

Chart Legend

☐ K on RS, P on WS ╱ K2tog

⊙ YO ╲ Ssk

BUTTERFLIES

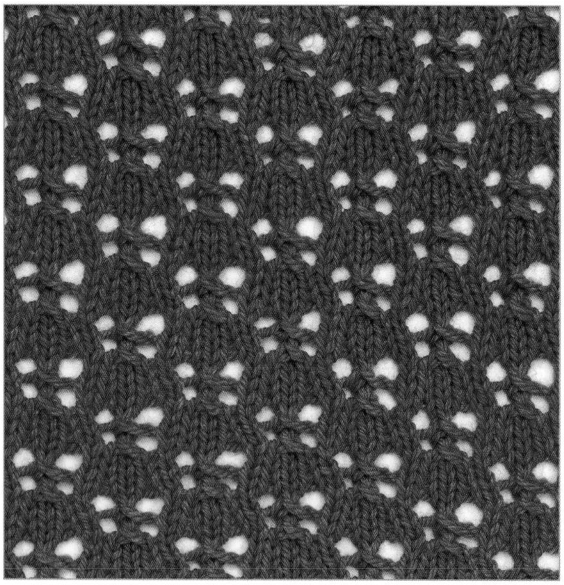

WRITTEN INSTRUCTIONS FOR BUTTERFLIES CHART

If you prefer to follow row-by-row instructions rather than a chart, use the instructions that follow. If you are using stitch markers to mark each lace repeat on the charts, you'll need to rearrange your stitch markers on rows 5, 7, 13, and 15.

Row 1 (RS): YO, K1, *K2, YO, sk2p, YO, K3; rep from * to marker, YO.

Row 2 and all even-numbered rows (WS): Purl all sts.

Row 3: YO, K2, *K2, YO, sk2p, YO, K3; rep from * to 1 st before marker, K1, YO.

Row 5: YO, K1, YO, sk2p, *YO, K5, YO, sk2p; rep from * to 1 st before marker, YO, K1, YO.

Row 7: YO, K2, YO, sk2p, *YO, K5, YO, sk2p; rep from * to 2 sts before marker, YO, K2, YO.

Row 9: YO, K5, *K2, YO, sk2p, YO, K3; rep from * to 4 sts before marker, K4, YO.

Row 11: YO, K1, K2tog, YO, K3, *K2, YO, sk2p, YO, K3; rep from * to 5 sts before marker, K2, YO, ssk, K1, YO.

Row 13: YO, K5, YO, sk2p, *YO, K5, YO, sk2p; rep from * to 5 sts before marker, YO, K5, YO.

Row 15: YO, K6, YO, sk2p, *YO, K5, YO, sk2p; rep from * to 6 sts before marker, YO, K6, YO.

Row 16: Purl all sts.

Rep rows 1–16 for patt.

Wedge Shawl Template: Butterflies Chart

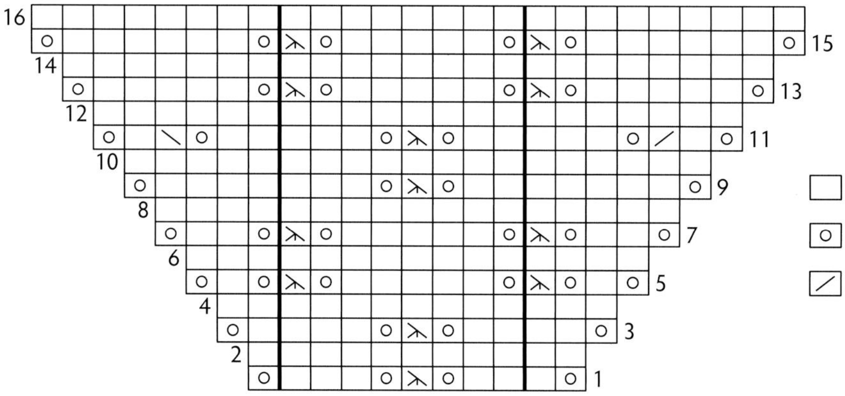

Repeat = 8 sts

Chart Legend

- K on RS, P on WS
- YO
- K2tog
- Ssk
- Sk2p

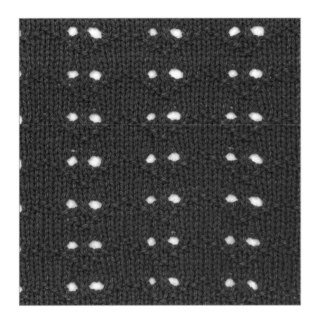

WRITTEN INSTRUCTIONS FOR ZIGZAGS WITH EYELETS CHART

If you prefer to follow row-by-row instructions rather than a chart, use the instructions below.

Row 1 (RS): YO, K1, *K3, P1, K4; rep from * to marker, YO.

Row 2 (WS): P1, *P3, K1, P1, K1, P2; rep from * to 2 sts before marker, P2.

Row 3: YO, K2, *K1, P1, K3, P1, K2; rep from * to 1 st before marker, K1, YO.

Row 4: P2, *P1, K1, P5, K1; rep from * to 3 sts before marker, P3.

Row 5: YO, K2, P1, *K2, YO, cdd, YO, K2, P1; rep from * to 2 sts before marker, K2, YO.

Row 6: Purl all sts.

Row 7: YO, knit to marker, YO.

Row 8: Purl all sts.

Row 9: YO, P1, K4, *K3, P1, K4; rep from * to 4 sts before marker, K3, P1, YO.

Row 10: P2, K1, P2, *P3, K1, P1, K1, P2; rep from * to 6 sts before marker, P3, K1, P2.

Row 11: YO, K3, P1, K2, *K1, P1, K3, P1, K2; rep from * to 5 sts before marker, K1, P1, K3, YO.

Row 12: P5, K1, *P1, K1, P5, K1; rep from * to 7 sts before marker, P1, K1, P5.

Row 13: YO, K1, YO, cdd, YO, K2, P1, *K2, YO, cdd, YO, K2, P1; rep from * to 6 sts before marker, K2, YO, cdd, YO, K1, YO.

Row 14: Purl all sts.

Row 15: Rep row 7.

Row 16: Purl all sts.

Rep rows 1–16 for patt.

Wedge Shawl Template: Zigzags with Eyelets Chart

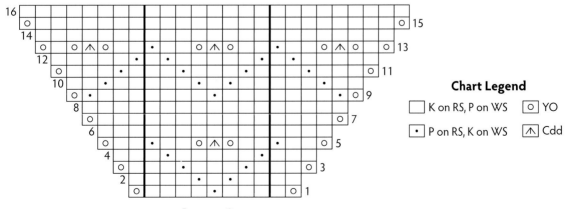

Repeat = 8 sts

Chart Legend

☐ K on RS, P on WS ⊙ YO

• P on RS, K on WS ⋀ Cdd

Row 3: YO, K2, *YO, K2, cdd, K2, YO, K1; rep from * to 1 st before marker, K1, YO.

Row 5: YO, K3, *YO, K2, cdd, K2, YO, K1; rep from * to 2 sts before marker, K2, YO.

Row 7: YO, K4, *YO, K2, cdd, K2, YO, K1; rep from * to 3 sts before marker, K3, YO.

Row 9: YO, K2, K2tog, YO, K1, *YO, K2, cdd, K2, YO, K1; rep from * to 4 sts before marker, YO, ssk, K2, YO.

Row 11: YO, K2, K2tog, K1, YO, K1, *YO, K2, cdd, K2, YO, K1; rep from * to 5 sts before marker, YO, K1, ssk, K2, YO.

Row 13: YO, K2, K2tog, K2, YO, K1, *YO, K2, cdd, K2, YO, K1; rep from * to 6 sts before marker, YO, K2, ssk, K2, YO.

Row 15: YO, K3, K2tog, K2, YO, K1, *YO, K2, cdd, K2, YO, K1; rep from * to 7 sts before marker, YO, K2, ssk, K3, YO.

Row 16: Purl all sts.

Rep row 1–16 for patt.

WRITTEN INSTRUCTIONS FOR EYELET LADDERS CHART

If you prefer to follow row-by-row instructions rather than a chart, use the instructions below.

Row 1 (RS): YO, K1, *YO, K2, cdd, K2, YO, K1; rep from * to marker, YO.

Row 2 and all even-numbered rows (WS): Purl all sts.

Wedge Shawl Template: Eyelet Ladders Chart

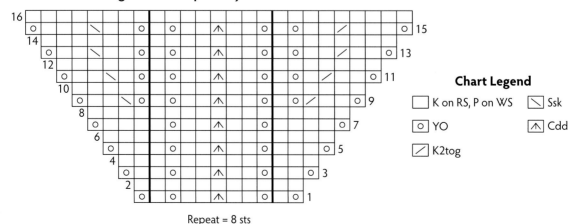

Repeat = 8 sts

Chart Legend

☐ K on RS, P on WS		◣ Ssk
◉ YO		⋀ Cdd
⟋ K2tog		

WRITTEN INSTRUCTIONS FOR EYELET MESH CHART

If you prefer to follow row-by-row instructions rather than a chart, use the instructions below.

Row 1 (RS): YO, K1, *YO, cdd, YO, K1; rep from * to marker, YO.

Row 2 and all even-numbered rows (WS): Purl all sts.

Row 3: YO, K2, *YO, cdd, YO, K1; rep from * to 1 st before marker, K1, YO.

Row 5: YO, K3, *YO, cdd, YO, K1; rep from * to 2 sts before marker *, K2, YO.

Row 7: YO, K4, *YO, cdd, YO, K1; rep from * to 3 sts before marker, K3, YO.

Row 9: Rep row 1.

Row 11: Rep row 3.

Row 13: Rep row 5.

Row 15: Rep row 7.

Row 16: Purl all sts.

Rep row 1–16 for patt.

Wedge Shawl Template: Eyelet Mesh Chart

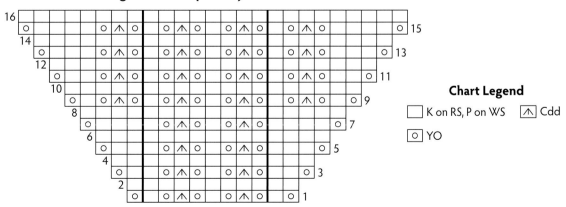

Repeat = 8 sts

Chart Legend

☐ K on RS, P on WS   ⅄ Cdd

⊡ YO

Crescent Shawls

🌙 *The crescent shawl has grown in popularity over the last few years. I think this is because it's so easy to wear; you can wrap it around yourself like a traditional shawl or turn it around and wear it as a scarf.*

Unlike wedge shawls, the tip of the shawl can't point to an area of your body that you don't want to show off. There's no harsh point, just a beautiful, gently curved edge that flatters, as in the Digitalis shawl (page 41) shown above.

Use the Crescent-Shawl Template below with any of the six stitch patterns on pages 77–84 to create a beautiful crescent shawl.

CRESCENT SHAWL TEMPLATE

Work garter tab CO (page 93) as foll: CO 2 sts. Knit 16 rows. Turn work 90° and pick up 8 sts along the edge. Turn work 90° and pick up 2 sts from CO edge—12 sts total.

Set-up row (WS): K3, (YO, K1) to last 3 sts, YO, K3—19 sts.

Body of Shawl

Now you can start working lace st patts. Pick a st patt! Once you have worked the full st patt, you can work a different st patt or work the same one again. It's your shawl—it's up to you! Work shawl to desired length.

Make It Your Own!

All the stitch patterns in this section are a multiple of 12 stitches plus 1, so you can mix and match the patterns easily. Whichever st patt you choose to use, be sure to work the full st patt before moving on to the next one.

Finishing

BO loosely knitwise (page 94) on RS. Block shawl. With tapestry needle, weave in ends.

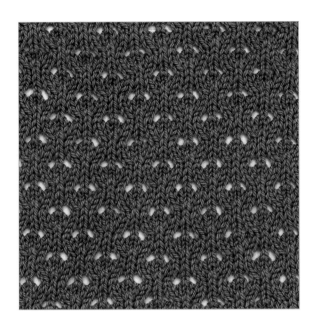

WRITTEN INSTRUCTIONS FOR LYRE LACE CHART

If you prefer to follow row-by-row instructions rather than a chart, use the instructions below.

Row 1 (RS): K2, (YO, K1) twice, *YO, K1, cdd, K1, YO, K1; rep from * to last 3 sts, YO, K1, YO, K2.

Row 2 and all even-numbered rows (WS): K3, YO, K1, purl to last 4 sts, K1, YO, K3.

Row 3: K2, YO, K1, YO, knit to last 3 sts, YO, K1, YO, K2.

Row 5: K2, YO, K1, YO, K4, YO, K1, cdd, *(K1, YO) twice, K1, cdd; rep from * to last 8 sts, K1, YO, K4, YO, K1, YO, K2.

Row 7: Rep row 3.

Row 8: K3, YO, K1, purl to last 4 sts, K1, YO, K3.

Rep rows 1–8 for patt.

Crescent Shawl Template: Lyre Lace Chart

Repeat = 12 sts

Chart Legend

☐ K on RS, P on WS   ○ YO

• P on RS, K on WS   ⋏ Cdd

WRITTEN INSTRUCTIONS FOR FIELD OF BLOSSOMS CHART

If you prefer to follow row-by-row instructions rather than a chart, use the instructions below.

Row 1 (RS): K2, YO, K1, YO, knit to last 3 sts, YO, K1, YO, K2.

Row 2 and all even-numbered rows (WS): K3, YO, K1, purl to last 4 sts, K1, YO, K3.

Row 3: K2, YO, K1, YO, K2, YO, cdd, *YO, K3, YO, cdd; rep from * to last 5 sts, YO, K2, YO, K1, YO, K2.

Row 5: K2, (YO, K1) twice, *YO, K2tog, K1, ssk, YO, K1; rep from * to last 3 sts, YO, K1, YO, K2.

Row 7: Rep row 1.

Row 9: Rep row 3.

Row 11: K2, YO, K1, YO, K4, *ssk, YO, K1, YO, K2tog, K1; rep from * to last 6 sts, K3, YO, K1, YO, K2.

Row 13: Rep row 1.

Row 15: Rep row 3.

Row 17: Rep row 5.

Row 19: Rep row 1.

Row 21: Rep row 3.

Row 23: Rep row 11.

Row 24: K3, YO, K1, purl to last 4 sts, K1, YO, K3.

Rep rows 1–24 for patt.

Crescent Shawl Template: Field of Blossoms Chart

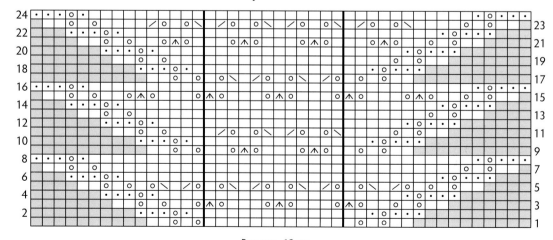

Repeat =12 sts

Chart Legend

☐ K on RS, P on WS ⊙ YO ◥ Ssk ▨ No stitch

▪ P on RS, K on WS ◿ K2tog ⋀ Cdd

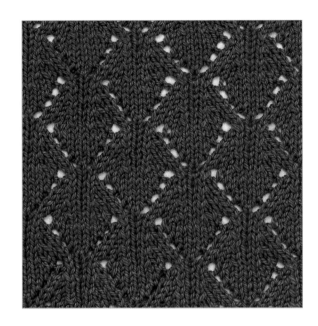

WRITTEN INSTRUCTIONS FOR LACE DIAMONDS CHART

If you prefer to follow row-by-row instructions rather than a chart, use the instructions below.

Row 1 (RS): K2, (YO, K1) twice, *YO, K3, K2tog, K1, ssk, K3, YO, K1; rep from * to last 3 sts, YO, K1, YO, K2.

Row 2 and all even-numbered rows (WS): K3, YO, K1, purl to last 4 sts, K1, YO, K3.

Row 3: K2, YO, K1, YO, K4, *K1, YO, K2, K2tog, K1, ssk, K2, YO, K2; rep from * to last 6 sts, K3, YO, K1, YO, K2.

Row 5: K2, (YO, K1) twice, ssk, K1, YO, K3, *K2, YO, K1, K2tog, K1, ssk, K1, YO, K3; rep from * to last 9 sts, K2, YO, K1, K2tog, (K1, YO) twice, K2.

Row 7: K2, YO, K1, YO, K4, ssk, YO, K4, *K3, YO, K2tog, K1, ssk, YO, K4; rep from * to last 12 sts, K3, YO, K2tog, K4, YO, K1, YO, K2.

Row 9: K2, (YO, K1) twice, *ssk, K3, YO, K1, YO, K3, K2tog, K1; rep from * to last 3 sts, YO, K1, YO, K2.

Row 11: K2, YO, K1, YO, K4, *ssk, K2, YO, K3, YO, K2, K2tog, K1; rep from * to last 6 sts, K3, YO, K1, YO, K2.

Row 13: K2, YO, K1, YO, K3, YO, K1, K2tog, K1, *ssk, K1, YO, K5, YO, K1, K2tog, K1; rep from * to last 9 sts, ssk, K1, YO, K3, YO, K1, YO, K2.

Row 15: K2, YO, K1, YO, K7, YO, K2tog, K1, *ssk, YO, K7, YO, K2tog, K1; rep from * to last 12 sts, ssk, YO, K7, YO, K1, YO, K2.

Row 16: K3, YO, K1, purl to last 4 sts, K1, YO, K3.

Rep rows 1–16 for patt.

Crescent Shawl Template: Lace Diamonds Chart

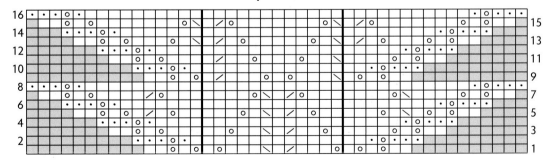

Repeat = 12 sts

Chart Legend

☐ K on RS, P on WS	○ YO	� figure Ssk
• P on RS, K on WS	⟋ K2tog	▨ No stitch

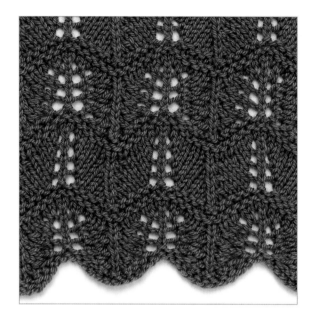

WRITTEN INSTRUCTIONS FOR CHEVRON-RIDGE LACE CHART

If you prefer to follow row-by-row instructions rather than a chart, use the instructions below.

Row 1 (RS): K2, (YO, K1) twice, *(YO, K1) twice, ssk, cdd, K2tog, (K1, YO) twice, K1; rep from * to last 3 sts, YO, K1, YO, K2.

Row 2 (WS): K3, YO, K1, purl to last 4 sts, K1, YO, K3.

Row 3: K2, YO, K1, YO, K4, *(YO, K1) twice, ssk, cdd, K2tog, (K1, YO) twice, K1; rep from * to last 6 sts, K3, YO, K1, YO, K2.

Row 4: Rep row 2.

Row 5: K2, YO, K1, YO, K3, K2tog, K1, YO, K1, *(YO, K1) twice, ssk, cdd, K2tog, (K1, YO) twice, K1; rep from * to last 9 sts, YO, K1, ssk, K3, YO, K1, YO, K2.

Row 6: Rep row 2.

Row 7: K2, YO, K1, YO, K3, K2tog twice, (K1, YO) twice, K1, *(YO, K1) twice, ssk, cdd, K2tog, (K1, YO) twice, K1; rep from * to last 12 sts, (YO, K1) twice, ssk twice, K3, YO, K1, YO, K2.

Row 8: Rep row 2.

Row 9: K2, YO, K1, YO, knit to last 3 sts, YO, K1, YO, K2.

Row 10: K3, YO, knit to last 3 sts, YO, K3.

Row 11: Rep row 9.

Row 12: Rep row 10.

Row 13: K2, (YO, K1) twice, K2tog, K3, YO, K1, *YO, K4, cdd, K4, YO, K1; rep from * to last 9 sts, YO, K3, ssk, (K1, YO) twice, K2.

Row 14: Rep row 2.

Row 15: K2, YO, K1, YO, K3, K2tog, K4, YO, K1, *YO, K4, cdd, K4, YO, K1; rep from * to last 12 sts, YO, K4, ssk, K3, YO, K1, YO, K2.

Row 16: Rep row 2.

Row 17: K2, (YO, K1) twice, *YO, K4, cdd, K4, YO, K1; rep from * to last 3 sts, YO, K1, YO, K2.

Row 18: Rep row 2.

Row 19: K2, YO, K1, YO, K4, *YO, K4, cdd, K4, YO, K1; rep from * to last 6 sts, K3, YO, K1, YO, K2.

Row 20: Rep row 2.

Row 21: Rep row 9.

Row 22: Rep row 10.

Row 23: Rep row 9.

Row 24: Rep row 10.

Rep rows 1–24 for patt.

Crescent Shawl Template: Chevron-Ridge Lace Chart

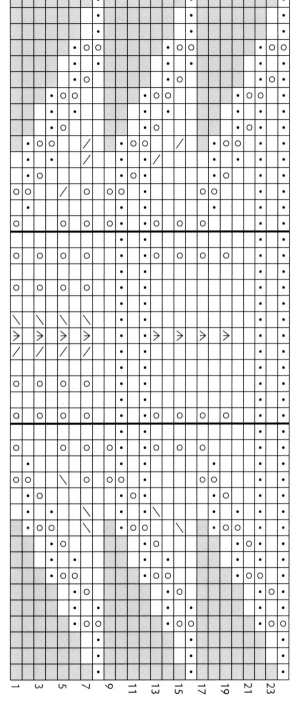

Repeat = 12 sts

Chart Legend

☐	K on RS, P on WS
•	P on RS, K on WS
○	YO
╱	K2tog
╲	Ssk
⋏	Cdd
▨	No stitch

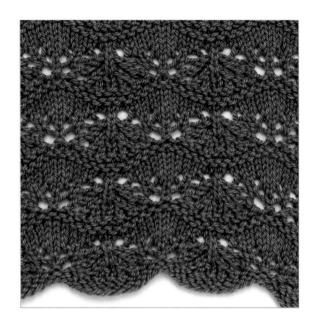

WRITTEN INSTRUCTIONS FOR SHELLS CHART

If you prefer to follow row-by-row instructions rather than a chart, use the instructions below.

Row 1 (RS): K2, (YO, K1) twice, *YO, K1, YO, ssk twice, K1, K2tog twice, (YO, K1) twice; rep from * to last 3 sts, YO, K1, YO, K2.

Row 2 (WS): K3, YO, K1, purl to last 4 sts, K1, YO, K3.

Row 3: K2, YO, K1, YO, K4, *YO, K1, YO, ssk twice, K1, K2tog twice, (YO, K1) twice; rep from * to last 6 sts, K3, YO, K1, YO, K2.

Row 4: Rep row 2.

Row 5: K2, YO, K1, YO, K2, K2tog, K1, YO, K2, *(K1, YO) twice, ssk, cdd, K2tog, YO, K1, YO, K2; rep from * to last 9 sts, K1, YO, K1, ssk, K2, YO, K1, YO, K2.

Row 6: Rep row 2.

Row 7: K2, YO, K1, YO, K2, YO, cdd, YO, K5, *K4, YO, cdd, YO, K5; rep from * to last 12 sts, K4, YO, cdd, YO, K2, YO, K1, YO, K2.

Row 8: Rep row 2.

Row 9: K2, YO, K1, YO, knit to last 3 sts, YO, K1, YO, K2.

Row 10: K3, YO, knit to last 3 sts, YO, K3.

Row 11: Rep row 9.

Row 12: Rep row 10.

Row 13: K2, YO, K1, YO, K3, K2tog, K1, YO, K1, *YO, K1, YO, ssk twice, K1, K2tog twice, (YO, K1) twice; rep from * to last 9 sts, YO, K1, ssk, K3, YO, K1, YO, K2.

Row 14: Rep row 2.

Row 15: K2, YO, K1, YO, K4, K2tog twice, (YO, K1) twice, *YO, K1, YO, ssk twice, K1, K2tog twice, (YO, K1) twice; rep from * to last 12 sts, YO, K1, YO, ssk twice, K4, YO, K1, YO, K2.

Row 16: Rep row 2.

Row 17: K2, (YO, K1) twice, *(K1, YO) twice, ssk, cdd, K2tog, YO, K1, YO, K2; rep from * to last 3 sts, YO, K1, YO, K2.

Row 18: Rep row 2.

Row 19: K2, YO, K1, YO, K4, *K4, YO, cdd, YO, K5; rep from * to last 6 sts, K3, YO, K1, YO, K2.

Row 20: Rep row 2.

Row 21: Rep row 9.

Row 22: Rep row 10.

Row 23: Rep row 9.

Row 24: Rep row 10.

Rep rows 1–24 for patt.

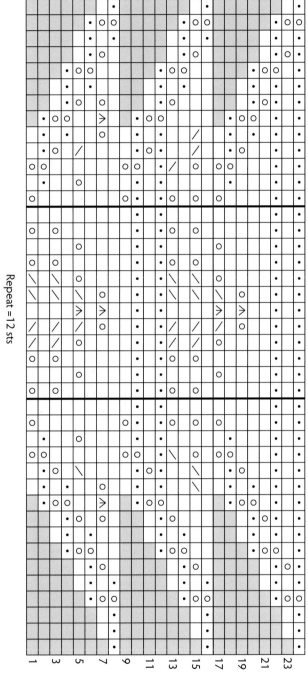

Repeat = 12 sts

Chart Legend

	K on RS, P on WS		Ssk
	P on RS, K on WS		Cdd
	YO		No stitch
	K2tog		

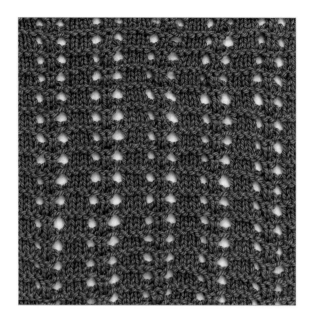

WRITTEN INSTRUCTIONS FOR RIDGE-AND-EYELET LADDERS CHART

If you prefer to follow row-by-row instructions rather than a chart, use the instructions below.

Row 1 (RS): K2, YO, K1, YO, knit to last 3 sts, YO, K1, YO, K2.

Row 2 (WS): K3, YO, K1, purl to last 4 sts, K1, YO, K3.

Row 3: K2, YO, K1, YO, K4, *K1, YO, cdd, YO, K3, YO, cdd, YO, K2; rep from * to last 6 sts, K3, YO, K1, YO, K2.

Row 4: K3, YO, knit to last 3 sts, YO, K3.

Rows 5–8: Rep rows 1–4.

Rep rows 1–8 for patt.

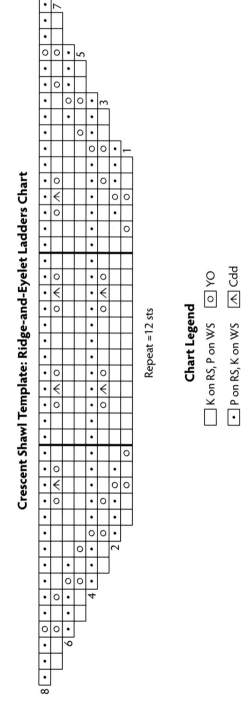

Crescent Shawl Template: Ridge-and-Eyelet Ladders Chart

Repeat =12 sts

Chart Legend

☐ K on RS, P on WS   ☐ YO

· P on RS, K on WS   ⋀ Cdd

Top-Down Shawls

Half-Circle Shawls

The half-circle shawl is a fun shawl shape to knit and to wear. Based on the pi shawl invented by Elizabeth Zimmermann, this shawl uses the same mathematic principles.

There are many advantages to half-circle shawls. Since all the increasing happens in one dedicated increase row, you don't have to worry about increasing while simultaneously working a lace pattern. These shawls stay on the shoulders nicely—they tend to wrap a bit like a crescent shawl, as you can see for the Nymans shawl (page 63) shown above, although they typically have greater depth.

Use the Half-Circle Shawl Template at right and any of the six stitch patterns on pages 87–92 to create a gorgeous half-circle shawl of your own!

HALF-CIRCLE SHAWL TEMPLATE

Work garter tab CO (page 93) as foll: CO 3 sts. Knit 22 rows. Turn work 90° and pick up 11 sts along the edge. Turn work 90° and pick up 3 sts from CO edge—17 sts total.

Beginning Section

Set-up row (WS): Knit all sts.

Inc row (RS): K3, (K1, YO) to last 4 sts, K4—27 sts.

Row 2: K3, purl to last 3 sts, K3.

Row 3: Knit all sts.

Row 4: Rep row 2.

Work inc row—47 sts.

Row 6: K3, purl to last 3 sts, K3.

Row 7: Knit all sts.

Rep rows 6 and 7 twice more. Rep row 6 once more.

Make It Your Own!

All the stitch patterns in this section are a multiple of 10 + 1 stitches wide. If you are picking a pattern from a stitch dictionary, you'll need to create a chart that accounts for the 3 stitches on each edge that are worked in garter stitch.

Lace Patterns

Work inc row—87 sts.

Next row: K3, purl to last 3 sts, K3.

Work desired st patt(s) for a total of 16 rows.

Work inc row—167 sts.

Next row: K3, purl to last 3 sts, K3.

Work desired st patt(s) for a total of 32 rows.

Work inc row—327 sts.

Next row: K3, purl to last 3 sts, K3.

Work desired st patt(s) for a total of 48 rows.

More Options!

Running out of yarn on the last section? No worries! Just knit until you have enough yarn to bind off. Want an even larger shawl? Work the increase row and next row, and then work desired stitch pattern(s) for 96 rows, or to desired length.

FINISHING

BO loosely knitwise (page 94) on RS. Block shawl. With tapestry needle, weave in ends.

WRITTEN INSTRUCTIONS FOR WAVES CHART

If you prefer to follow row-by-row instructions rather than a chart, use the instructions below.

Row 1 (RS): K4, *YO, ssk, K5, K2tog, YO, K1; rep from * to last 3 sts, K3.

Row 2 and all even-numbered rows (WS): K3, purl to last 3 sts, K3.

Row 3: K4, *K1, YO, ssk, K3, K2tog, YO, K2; rep from * to last 3 sts, K3.

Row 5: K4, *K2, YO, ssk, K1, K2tog, YO, K3; rep from * to last 3 sts, K3.

Row 7: K4, *K3, YO, cdd, YO, K4; rep from * to last 3 sts, K3.

Row 9: K4, *K1, K2tog, (K1, YO) twice, K1, ssk, K2; rep from * to last 3 sts, K3.

Rows 11, 13, and 15: Rep row 9.

Row 16: K3, purl to last 3 sts, K3.

Rep rows 1–16 for patt.

Half-Circle Shawl Template: Waves Chart

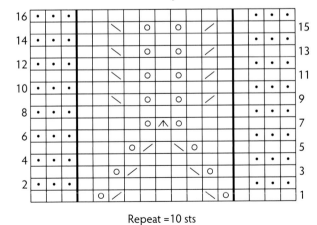

Repeat = 10 sts

Chart Legend

☐ K on RS, P on WS   ╱ K2tog

• P on RS, K on WS   ╲ Ssk

○ YO   ⋏ Cdd

WRITTEN INSTRUCTIONS FOR TEXTURED-LACE DIAMONDS CHART

If you prefer to follow row-by-row instructions rather than a chart, use the instructions below.

Row 1 (RS): K4, *YO, ssk, P5, K2tog, YO, K1; rep from * to last 3 sts, K3.

Row 2 (WS): K3, *P3, K5, P2; rep from * to last 4 sts, P1, K3.

Row 3: K4, *K1, YO, ssk, P3, K2tog, YO, K2; rep from * to last 3 sts, K3.

Row 4: K3, *P4, K3, P3; rep from * to last 4 sts, P1, K3.

Row 5: K4, *K2, YO, ssk, P1, K2tog, YO, K3; rep from * to last 3 sts, K3.

Row 6: K3, *P5, K1, P4; rep from * to last 4 sts, P1, K3.

Row 7: K4, *K4, P1, K5; rep from * to last 3 sts, K3.

Row 8: K3, *K4, P3, K3; rep from * to last 4 sts, K4.

Row 9: K3, P1, *P2, K2tog, YO, K1, YO, ssk, P3; rep from * to last 3 sts, K3.

Row 10: K3, *K3, P5, K2; rep from * to last 4 sts, K4.

Row 11: K3, P1, *P1, K2tog, YO, K3, YO, ssk, P2; rep from * to last 3 sts, K3.

Row 12: K3, *K2, P7, K1; rep from * to last 4 sts, K4.

Row 13: K3, P1, *K2tog, YO, K5, YO, ssk, P1; rep from * to last 3 sts, K3.

Row 14: K3, *K1, P9; rep from * to last 4 sts, K4.

Row 15: K3, P1, *K9, P1; rep from * to last 3 sts, K3.

Row 16: K3, *P2, K7, P1; rep from * to last 4 sts, P1, K3.

Rep rows 1–16 for patt.

Half-Circle Shawl Template: Textured-Lace Diamonds Chart

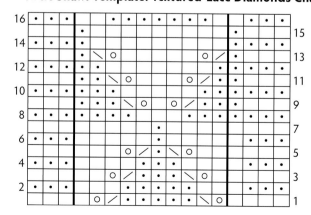

Repeat =10 sts

Chart Legend

☐ K on RS, P on WS	⟋ K2tog
• P on RS, K on WS	⟍ Ssk
○ YO	

WRITTEN INSTRUCTIONS FOR VERTICAL ZIGZAGS CHART

If you prefer to follow row-by-row instructions rather than a chart, use the instructions below.

Row 1 (RS): K4, *K1, K2tog, YO, K3, YO, ssk, K2; rep from * to last 3 sts, K3.

Row 2 and all even-numbered rows (WS): K3, purl to last 3 sts, K3.

Row 3: K4, *K2tog, YO, K5, YO, ssk, K1; rep from * to last 3 sts, K3.

Row 5: K4, *K2, YO, ssk, K1, K2tog, YO, K3; rep from * to last 3 sts, K3.

Row 7: K4, *K3, YO, cdd, YO, K4; rep from * to last 3 sts, K3.

Row 8: K3, purl to last 3 sts, K3.

Rep rows 1–8 for patt.

Half-Circle Shawl Template: Vertical Zigzags Chart

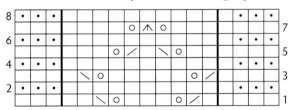

Repeat =10 sts

Chart Legend

☐	K on RS, P on WS	╱	K2tog
•	P on RS, K on WS	╲	Ssk
○	YO	⋀	Cdd

WRITTEN INSTRUCTIONS FOR HORSESHOE LACE CHART

If you prefer to follow row-by-row instructions rather than a chart, use the instructions below.

Row 1 (RS): K4, *YO, K3, cdd, K3, YO, K1; rep from * to last 3 sts, K3.

Row 2 and all even-numbered rows (WS): K3, purl to last 3 sts, K3.

Row 3: K4, *K1, YO, K2, cdd, K2, YO, K2; rep from * to last 3 sts, K3.

Row 5: K4, *K2, YO, K1, cdd, K1, YO, K3; rep from * to last 3 sts, K3.

Row 7: K4, *K3, YO, cdd, YO, K4; rep from * to last 3 sts, K3.

Row 8: K3, purl to last 3 sts, K3.

Rep rows 1–8 for patt.

Half-Circle Shawl Template: Horseshoe Lace Chart

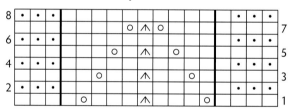

Repeat = 10 sts

Chart Legend

☐ K on RS, P on WS   ⊙ YO

▢ P on RS, K on WS   ⅄ Cdd

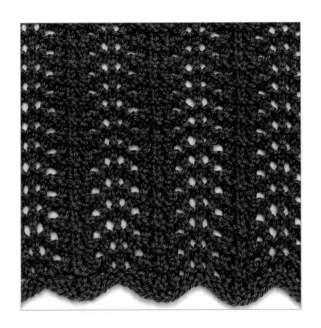

WRITTEN INSTRUCTIONS FOR FEATHER AND FAN VARIATION CHART

This feather-and-fan pattern features a cdd-central double decrease. If you prefer to follow row-by-row instructions rather than a chart, use the instructions below.

Row 1 (RS): K4, *YO, K1, YO, ssk, cdd, K2tog, (YO, K1) twice; rep from * to last 3 sts, K3.

Row 2 (WS): K3, purl to last 3 sts, K3.

Rows 3 and 4: Knit all sts.

Rep rows 1–4 for patt.

Half-Circle Shawl Template: Feather and Fan Variation Chart

Repeat =10 sts

Chart Legend

☐	K on RS, P on WS	⟋	K2tog
•	P on RS, K on WS	⟍	Ssk
○	YO	⋀	Cdd

WRITTEN INSTRUCTIONS FOR CHEVRON LADDERS CHART

If you prefer to follow row-by-row instructions rather than a chart, use the instructions below.

Row 1 (RS): K4, *YO, K3, cdd, K3, YO, K1; rep from * to last 3 sts, K3.

Row 2 (WS): K3, purl to last 3 sts, K3.

Rep rows 1 and 2 for patt.

Half-Circle Shawl Template: Chevron Ladders Chart

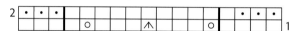

Repeat = 10 sts

Chart Legend

☐ K on RS, P on WS   ⊡ YO

⊡ P on RS, K on WS   ⋀ Cdd

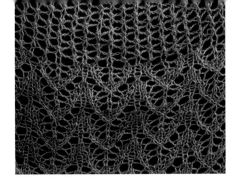

Special Techniques

The following techniques are used throughout the book and will help you successfully knit your projects.

GARTER TAB CAST ON

All the shawls in this book begin with a garter tab cast on. While the number of stitches will vary depending on the pattern, this cast on is typically worked as follows:

1. Cast on three stitches and knit six rows.

2. Rotate work clockwise 90° and pick up three stitches evenly along the edge by inserting the needle into each of the three garter stitch bumps on the left edge of the tab, from left to right, and then knit them.

3. Rotate work clockwise 90° and pick up and knit three stitches evenly from the cast-on edge (nine stitches total). Turn your work and continue with the next row of the pattern.

KNITWISE BIND OFF

For a shawl, the goal is to have a bind off that's stretchy so that when blocking, you can pull and form the edge any way you like. If you have a tendency to bind off tightly, use a needle one or two sizes larger.

To work, knit the first two stitches together through the back loop. *Slip the stitch from the right needle to the left needle with the yarn in back and knit two stitches together through the back loop; repeat from * until all stitches are bound off.

BLOCKING

Blocking supplies are kind of like knitting needles—everyone has their own personal preference. Here's a list of blocking supplies you might find useful:

- Wool wash

- Blocking mats

- Towel

- Blocking wires

- Rust-proof straight or T-pins

To block your shawl, place in a bath of lukewarm water, along with your favorite wool wash, if desired. Let the shawl soak and become completely saturated with water. Remove shawl from water, wrap it in a towel, and gently squeezing out excess water (do not twist or ring the towel). Place shawl on blocking mats or other flat surface you can pin on, and shape to finished measurements given in pattern, or to desired size. Be sure to accentuate the edge of the shawl—pull out the natural points in the lace and pin at the point. Let shawl completely dry in place.

Useful Information

For information including handy tables outlining skill levels, yarn weights, knitting-needle sizes, and metric conversions, go to ShopMartingale.com/TopDownShawls.

Abbreviations and Glossary

( ) Work instructions within parentheses in the place directed.

[ ] Work instructions within brackets in the place directed.

* Repeat instructions following the single asterisk as directed.

" inch(es)

beg begin(ning)

BO bind off

cdd Slip 2 stitches together as if to knit. Knit 1. Pass the slipped stitches over the knit stitch—2 sts decreased.

CO cast on

foll follow(ing)

g gram(s)

inc increase(ing)

K knit

K2tog Knit 2 stitches together—1 stitch decreased.

K3tog Knit 3 stitches together—1 stitch decreased.

kw knitwise

m meter(s)

mm millimeter(s)

oz ounce(s)

P purl

patt pattern

PM place marker

rep repeat

RS right side(s)

sk2p Slip 1 stitch purlwise, k2tog, pass slipped stitch over k2tog—2 stitches decreased.

sl slip

SM slip marker

ssk Slip 2 stitches knitwise, one at a time, to right needle, then insert left needle from left to right into front loops and knit 2 stitches together—1 stitch decreased.

sssk Slip 3 stitches knitwise, one at a time, to right needle, then insert needle from left to right into front loops and knit 3 stitches together—2 stitches decreased.

st(s) stitch(es)

WS wrong side(s)

yd(s) yard(s)

YO yarn over

Yarn Sources

Anzula Luxury Fibers
anzula.com
Cloud

Louet North America
louet.com
Gems Fingering

KnitCircus
knitcircus.com
Opulence

Lorna's Laces
lornaslaces.net
Shepherd Sport

Knit Picks
knitpicks.com
Hawthorne

The Fiber Seed
thefiberseed.com
Sprout DK

Sweet Georgia
sweetgeorgiayarns.com
CashLuxe Fine
Superwash DK

Malabrigo
malabrigoyarn.com
Baby Silkpaca

Stitch Sprouts
stitchsprouts.com
Yellowstone

Done Roving Yarns
doneroving.com
Frolicking Feet Transitions

Leading Men Fiber Arts
leadingmenfiberarts
.bigcartel.com
Diva

ACKNOWLEDGMENTS

Like every book I've written, this one wouldn't be possible without the amazing support team that helps me every step of the way. Thank you to my sample knitters: Rachel Brown, Jenni Lesniak, Cathy Rusk, and Melissa Rusk. You continue to amaze me with your incredible knitting skills.

Thank you to the entire Martingale team for once again being a wonderful group of people. I enjoy working with you on each and every book!

Finally, and most importantly, thank you to my husband, Alex, for continuing to support me and lift me up every day.

About the Author

Jen has been knitting since 2004 and designing since 2008. She's designed hundreds of patterns for books, magazines, and yarn companies, in addition to her growing self-published catalog online. When not knitting or crocheting, Jen can be found reading, cross-stitching, or taking a road trip. She lives in Fox River Grove, Illinois, with her husband, Alex.

FIND JEN ONLINE!

See Jen's designs at www.ravelry.com/designers/jen-lucas.
Check out Jen's website at www.jenlucasdesigns.com.
Follow Jen on Instagram @jenlucasdesigns.